BENNER'S PROPHECIES

OF

FUTURE UPS AND DOWNS IN PRICES.

WHAT YEARS TO MAKE MONEY ON PIG-IRON, HOGS, CORN,
AND PROVISIONS.

By SAMUEL BENNER,

An Ohio Farmer.

———

"I know of no way of judging of the future but by the past."
—PATRICK HENRY.

———

THIRD EDITION.

CINCINNATI:
ROBERT CLARKE & CO.
1884.

DEDICATED

There is a time in the price of certain
    products and commodities,
Which, if taken by men at the advance,
    leads on to fortune;
And if taken at the decline, leads to
    bankruptcy and ruin.

INDEX.

ADDENDA, 1884.

PREFACE.

IN the following pages the object of the writer is to give brief, full, and clear exposition of the ups and downs in prices for certain products and commodities in the markets of our country, to all who are struggling in the same for a competence.

To foresee the future intelligently in regard to supply and demand, production and consumption, is the great want that finance and commerce are to-day struggling and grappling with and striving to solve.

The question of prices will always be of great interest to the producer and consumer. The spirit of the age is tending toward speculation in the products of the "Farm, the Mine, and the Factory." All business operations for profit and future contracts are attended with a great deal of risk, and the leading branches of trade demand information on the subject, and that the uncertainties of the future be lessened.

There is always a hesitancy and a desire for further intelligence, in regard to engaging in any business where the chances for profit depend upon so many contingencies and circumstances.

The author, in presenting a practical book to the public on the subject, and on the branches of trade of which it treats, is inspired with the belief that it will be the greatest boon to the reader to have the years of high and low prices pointed out in the future.

It should be the highest aim of the farmer, manufacturer, and trader, in a business point of view, to penetrate the future and calculate what years he can realize the best prices for his products.

Content to be useful, instead of being voluminous, the writer has confined the book to a few of the most important branches of trade. To have extended the work to the dimensions of embracing other branches would have made it more copious than the designed brevity of the book would admit.

It is hoped that to this volume will be accorded the merit of directing more attention to the ups and downs in prices, and the causes producing and influencing the same.

And now, submitting the results of our labor, experience, and observation to the in dustry and commerce of the country, the author's wishes will be fully realized if this little volume contains any information which may be useful or of service to those interested

INTRODUCTION.

THE advance and decline in the average
price of pig-iron, hogs, corn, and provisions in the markets of our country, for a
series of twenty years past, and for certain
periods, have been as alternately certain as
the diurnal revolutions of the earth upon its
axis; and the periods of high and low prices
have been as regular in rotation, as the annual return of the four seasons.

Now, READER: You who may study the ups
and downs in prices as collated and considered in these pages, and operate in accordance
with the advance of prices and tendencies of
the times, as here indicated, will surely be
successful; whilst those who stubbornly and
blindly prosecute on the decline, will do an
unprofitable business, and will meet with continued disaster and loss.

I am well aware that my prediction of the
downward tendency in the prices of pig-iron,
hogs, corn, and provisions, and dull trade for
the next two years, will be to some as unwel-

(x)

come as the tolling of the-fire bell at the hour of midnight; and to others as unexpected as was the approach of the Medes and Persians, under the walls of Babylon, to the banquetors at the royal board of Belshazzar; but we can not be blamed for foretelling that which can not be averted and which past prices, and signs of the times indicate, and which a conscientious conviction of duty compels us to predict, with the hope that our premonition may serve to diminish disaster and save national and individual interests from ruin.

I now at once make my predictions, and will endeavor to demonstrate their certainty and fulfillment to the comprehension of all, by an examination of past prices, and their bearing upon the future, as analyzed by the light of practical experience and sound analogy.

PREDICTIONS.

PIG-IRON.

I PREDICT *that* the average price of No. 1 foundry charcoal pig-iron in the markets of our country will be lower in the year 1876 than in 1875.

I predict *that* the average price of No. 1 foundry charcoal pig-iron in the markets of our country will be lower in the year 1877 than in 1876, and *that* the daily price in some months of that year will run below twenty dollars per ton.

I predict *that* the average price of No. 1 foundry charcoal pig-iron in the markets of our country will be higher in the year 1878 than in 1877.

I predict *that* the average price of No. 1 foundry charcoal pig-iron in the markets of our country will be higher in the year 1879 than in 1878, notwithstanding the resumption of specie payments.

I predict *that* the average price of No. 1 foundry charcoal pig-iron in the markets of our country will be higher in the year 1880 than in 1879.

I predict *that* the average price of No. 1 foundry charcoal pig-iron in the markets of our country will be higher in the year 1881 than in 1880, and *that* the daily price in some months of that year will run above fifty dollars per ton.

The average prices as determined for the " American Iron and Steel Association."

HOGS.

I predict *that* the average price of fat hogs in the markets of our country will be lower in the year 1876 than in 1875.

I predict *that* the average price of fat hogs in the markets of our country will be lower in the year 1877 than in 1876.

I predict *that* the average price of fat hogs in the markets of our country will be higher in the year 1878 than in 1877.

I predict *that* the average price of fat hogs in the markets of our country will be higher in the year 1879 than in 1878, notwithstanding the resumption of specie payments.

I predict *that* the average price of fat hogs

iu the markets of our country will be higher in the year 1880 than in 1879.

The average prices as determined by the "CINCINNATI PRICE CURRENT."

PANIC.

I predict *that* there will be great depression in general business, and many failures in the years 1876 and 1877, and *that* there will be a commercial revulsion, and a financial crisis in the year 1891.

Here are twelve prophecies of certain events to take place in the future, and they are of no uncertain sound; either one of them, if taken advantage of, by large operators and speculators, would make and save them millions of money, and would be of incalculable benefit to every person in this country. To know *when* to shape our agricultural, manufacturing, and financial operations, so as to secure the best markets instead of the worst, is the end much to be desired by all.

These prophecies are made not upon supposed fanciful speculation, but from the testimony of twenty years' observation by the writer, from living and experienced facts; from the yearly average prices compiled by

recognized official authority, and by analogy, relying upon "history to repeat itself."

The writer does not claim a "gift of
prophecy," but he does claim a *Cast Iron Rule*
that will do to keep in sight, and that future
ups and downs of the markets, and high and
low prices in certain products and commodities, can be calculated for some years to come
with as much certainty, and upon the same
principle that an astronomer calculates an
eclipse of the sun.

It is not upon record that Joseph had
Egyptian weather statistics, or tables of production and prices, to base his prediction
and interpretation of Pharaoh's dream; but
he relied upon divine power to *fulfill* his
prophecy. On our part, we base our predictions upon the records of the past, and their
relation to the future, as governed by the unchangeable laws of nature, and only rely upon
providence for their *fulfillment* to give us the
continued regular progress and development
of these laws, and to its usual dispensation for
seasons to make large or small crops, and not
on the peoples' efforts merely.

The author firmly believes that God is ir
rices, and that the over and under produc-

tion of every commodity is in accordance
with his will, with strict reference to the
wants of mankind, and governed by the laws
of nature, which are God's laws; and that the
production, advance, and decline of average
prices should be systematic, and occur in an
established providential succession, as certain
and regular as the magnetic needle points un-
erringly to the pole.

Are not all kinds of business at loose ends—
astray, tossed on the tempestuous sea of uncertainty—from our imperfect knowledge of
natural causes and the laws by which they
operate; and our lack of accurate statistics
of production and prices, a knowledge of
which would enable us to discover and establish reliable rules for our guidance in the future? Is there any thing certain and settled
in farming, except that a broom-handle is a
sure cure for hoven in cattle! Are not farmers, furnace-men, manufacturers, traders and
speculators at random, like a ship without
compass or rudder? Do not all operations in
business depend for success upon a certain
number of fixed, reliable rules? The rules
we have to commence and transact business
upon are stereotyped rules, that "HONESTY is
the best policy;" that industry, energy, per-

severance, prudence, economy, and so on, lead
to riches and competence. These are all good
enough in their line, and indispensable to
success, but are they all-sufficient? Is this
knowledge all that is absolutely required for
successful business in every department of
trade? Is there not a knowledge of something more which a business man wants?
And who is not a business man? In order to
guide him in reference to future prices that
are to rule in the markets of our country,
we can not close our eyes and ignore the fact
that there is a want of rules by which to in-
terpret the "signs of the times," and to enable us to comprehend the future status of the
markets, so we may know six months or a
year ahead what are to be the conditions and
circumstances that will produce the coming
ups and downs in prices for any product or
commodity, and when the changes from high
and low prices are to take place.

How are we to get this information, this
insight into, or foresight of the future?

Do the Records of the Weather Give the Rule?

In seeking to forecast future prices of agricultural products, the weather is an impor-

tant element of uncertainty. With the rapidly increasing means of observation, and the
deep interest taken by governments and
scientists every-where in the laws of climate,
the development and path of storms, nature
of calms, theory of winds, movements of
masses of hot and dry air, and the phenomena of rain and snow, we may in time learn
to calculate with certainty what years will
be dry or wet; when we may expect years of
heat, storm, and cold; but with all the
weather statistics of the past, tables of meteorology, and not excepting the weather wisdom
of almanac makers, it will not come within
the province of this work to lay down rules
by which to forecast the future of the
weather. It will require time, research, with
improved means, and a more complete series
of meteorological and climatological observa-
tions to form a system of probabilities that
can be useful; and when the weather probabilities are reduced to a science, it will then
be a long step to determine agricultural productions and prices from them; and if the
time should come when the weather bureau
at Washington can predict twelve months
ahead instead of twenty-four hours, we can
then know in advance what the seasons are

to be, the number of bushels or pounds of any thing to be produced, what prices will rule; and we can all make money.

It will not be one of the points of this book to determine the *causes of things*, or the conditions and elements which will produce the coming ups and downs in prices; with these questions these prophecies have nothing to do; it will only come within its sphere to ascertain and point out the periodical return of effects, in the changes from high and low prices.

We know the effects as manifested in the ups and downs of average prices, and good and bad trade, and it seems as though there ought to be an established cause to produce results of so much certainty, periodicity, and alternate regularity.

The difficulty encountered in determining the causes producing the changes in production and prices is, that we are compelled to reason *a posteriori*, from effect to cause, and "what can we reason but from what we know." All original causes are invisible, and that which is rendered visible through development is an effect; the cause must exist antecedent to the effect. The manner in which causes and their laws operate to produce these

effects may be found in our solar system, upon
which we hereafter give some theories. All
nature is found to be the servant of law:
spring, summer, autumn, and winter succeed
each other in unchangeable regularity, and
the recurrences of the various convulsions of
nature are being determined on scientific
principles; none of these things happen by
chance, but all of them by some law which
will shortly be solved; and when the causes
producing the changes in the weather, and
the operations of their laws are better under-
stood, we may be then better able to discover
their influence on the state of business in
manufacture, trade, and commerce; then we
may be enabled to fathom the conditions and
elements that will produce the coming ups
and downs in prices which are to rule in the
markets of our country.

Do the Statistics of Production Give the Rule?

To ascertain when the changes from high
and low prices are to take place:
Who is it that can tell us what is to be the
production of corn, cotton, wheat, tobacco, or
any product that grows from the ground, and
is dependent upon the season for the life or

death of the plant? No one; after they have gathered and collected all the information obtainable in regard to the acreage to be planted or sown, the seasons make large or small crops, and not the farmers.

A cold, wet spring through the months of April, May, and June, is almost fatal to the corn, cotton, tobacco, and other plants. Also a dry, hot summer, has the effect to destroy the growing stocks. Floods and early frosts are great destroyers of the cereals in our northern latitudes; either one of these elements operating diminishes the number of pounds or bushels, and produces short crops; therefore, we can not beforehand determine what will be the production of any year by that which has been planted or sown.

Statistics of agricultural products or manufactured commodities are generally too late to be available for present use; they come after a person has made their investment or disposed of their property. Agricultural statistics, as generally compiled at Washington, tell the farmer the aggregate amount or number of bushels produced six months or a year after their crops have been harvested and sold.

Statistics of production, either estimated or

sold for consumption, are not sufficient to operate upon; one is too soon, the other too late.

Commercial estimates are too high.

The future can not be calculated upon intelligently by agricultural statistics. The reason why they are not reliable is, that they are not given in by farmers correct: one farmer will think it has something to do with taxes, and he will give them in low; another, to magnify the yield of his farm, and other purposes, will give them in high; therefore, they can not be a criterion for future calculation and prices.

Again, statistics of what has been produced may vary considerably from the available supply. We can not make any correct estimate or compile any statistics of what has been done with a crop. The corn crop of one year may not feed more than two-thirds of the stock that the crop would of another year.

Statistics of foreign exports are not to be depended upon. The estimated aggregate amount of the yearly production of any crop or manufactured commodity, does not from year to year approximate any regularity of increase or decrease that indicates future production; and therefore the course of future prices can not be determined by them.

Statistics are generally huge columns of figures, of which no one knows all the channels from whence they came, all the clerical errors in their compilation, and parties interested in their manipulation.

In attempting to explore and explain the elements in these statistical tables and problems of which people think are few and easily read, the real supply and demand will be as unfathomable as the waters of the briny deep.

Does the Price Give the Rule?

The price of any product is the exponent of the accumulated wisdom of the country in regard to the available supply and prospective demand for that product; and as the price advances or declines, so it indicates the surplus or deficit of any product or commodity.

The daily price is always known in the markets. There may be incidental causes, which are always producing slight and temporary fluctuations in value. The variation in price in one locality from another may be found in the cost of transportation or other local causes. The price is always known; the amount of any product and the demand for the same, is not so easily obtained. The books are always posted in regard to price, but several pages behind on amount of product available and the demand for the same. The price is the index of the probable amount of any product or commodity that is demanded for general consumption.

The price which an article will command to-morrow or next week can not always be known, as there are so many contingencies to cause temporary fluctuations in the markets. One or more of the various products may be manipulated so as to influence the price to advance or decline for a short time, but speculators can not influence any market only temporarily.

It is not within the wisdom of finite beings to comprehend all the temporary circumstances connected with prices, as governed and influenced by supply and demand, weather and seasons, combinations and corners, longs and shorts, puts and calls, and bulls and bears to operate upon the market.

Now as the temporary price is uncertain, let us look further into the subject of prices to find a rule, and take the average to ascertain if there is any regularity existing in the run of the markets. As prices of agricultural products are governed by production, and production is governed by the seasons, and as it takes the four seasons to determime the abundance or scarcity of a crop; therefore we are compelled to take the yearly average price to get above and beyond the control and influence of speculators, manipulators, and corners upon the market.

The yearly average price is ascertained by taking the price each day, week, or month, at one or more of the markets where the articles are bought and sold, and by adding the whole together, and then dividing by the number of times taken, the quotient will give the average for a year.

When the yearly average price is very low for any product or commodity, and next year advances, and so on until it reaches the highest average, is that which is here denominated an "*up?*" When the average price declines from one year to another to the lowest average, is that which is here denominated a "*down?*"

The "ups and downs" of yearly average prices, in a series of years for some articles, are very noticeable; and it can be observed that it takes a required number of years to complete an "up and down."

Now to find a rule that can give us any foresight of future markets, we must look to the past ups and downs of average prices; then ascertain how many years it takes to complete an up and down in any product or commodity, then determine in what order the ups and downs are repeated in the next cycle; and if there is found any noticeable periodicity in cycles, then we have a rule which can be applied to the future. An up and down or a down and up in average prices, is in this book denominated a cycle.

The cycles in yearly average prices

Gives Us The Rule.

The indubitable evidences and testimonies of observation have established this rule as the safest we have ever practiced and have ever found adapted to this purpose. And inside of this rule, like a wheel within a wheel, is to be found our "Cast Iron Rule," which is that *one extreme invariably follows another*, as can be witnessed in all the operations of nature, in all the business affairs of man, and in all the ramifications of trade and industry; and

in every cycle of average prices it is shown to
what extent these extremes run. This rule
when applied to pig-iron, hogs, corn and provisions, is as persistent as the attractive and re-
pulsive forces of the magnet, and as unchangeable as the laws of the Medes and Persians.

This knowledge of the years in which high
and low prices return in the markets, belong
to the farmer, manufacturer, and legitimate
trader, as well as the speculator; and it is as
important that this intelligence should be
known to one as to the other.

The ups and downs in prices, as considered
in this book, have reference to a series of years
as distinguished from the daily and weekly
fluctuations. War, panic, and elections have
not changed the general yearly course of prices
in some articles for many years past; and we
only go back so far as we have been enabled
to obtain reliable yearly average prices, or the
official records of monthly prices at New York,
and from them we can date their unfolding,
and since that time establish by our rule the
full development of our system of prophecy.

It is not necessary for us to look beyond the
present century, or to the history of prices in
older countries, for epochs of abundance and
scarcity, to prove recurring cycles in prices.

The alternation of good and bad harvests is well known in English history. "Tooke" published a history of prices in 1838, giving an exhaustive analysis of the causes producing abundance and scarcity in crops in the eighteenth century, but did not establish any rule by which the future course of prices could be arithmetically calculated.

It is to the present nineteenth century, and in the land of free America, the most favored nation upon the earth, that divine providence has arranged this matter, for not only the spread of the true principles of religion and liberty, but the full development of the operations of the unchangeable laws of nature around and about us.

The battles of Lexington, Concord and Bunker Hill, the centennial of which we celebrated in 1875, was the commencement of our struggles for freedom from the tyrannical yoke of England. The War of 1812 was the final consummation of our independence in the arts and sciences, commerce and politics; and the period in our history after which we can date the development of the reaper and mower, sewing-machine, grain elevator, power loom, cotton gin, stereotype, steam printing press, railroad, steamboat, electric telegraph, the compilation of average prices, new elements and sciences, and a multitude of inventions and discoveries for the advancement of man in his onward path of progress, and in the knowledge of the ways of an inscrutable providence.

Now instead of pondering over farmers' deliveries, weekly receipts, visible supplies, and entering into an expensive collection and elaborate examination of statistics of what the probable production of pig-iron, corn, and hogs will be, and the commercial demand for the same, and what old elements will be wanting and new ones to be developed, and watching and waiting to hear from New York, let us call history to the witness stand, and see what it has to testify on the subject; and also bring into court the testimony of observation and experience, by taking the course of the averages in past markets, as compiled by reliable and official authority; and also the years in which money has been made and lost in the different branches of trade, and then by our rule make the application for the future

PIG-IRON.

The following statement, prepared by Hon. Henry C. Carey, in 1849, embraces all that is definitely known of the progress of the iron industry in this country prior to 1854.

Mr. Carey's Pig-iron Statistics.

In 1810 the whole number of furnaces in the Union was 153, yielding 54,000 tons of metal, equal to 16 pounds per head of the population.

In 1821 the manufacture was in a state of ruin.

In 1828 the product had reached 130,000 tons, having little more than doubled in eighteen years.

In 1829 it was 142,000. Increase in one year nearly ten per cent.

In 1830 it was 165,000. Increase in two years more than 25 per cent.

In 1831 it was 191,000. Increase in three years about 50 per cent.

In 1832 it was 200,000, giving an increase in three years of above 60 per cent.

In 1840 the quantity given by the census was 286,000, but a committee of the Home League, in New York, made it 347,700 tons. Taking the medium of the two, it would give about 315,000 tons, being an increase in eight years of 50 per cent.

In 1842 a large portion of the furnaces were closed, and the product had fallen to probably little more than 200,000, but certainly less than 230,000 tons.

In 1846 it was estimated by the Secretary of the Treasury at 765,000 tons, having trebled in four years.

In 1847 it was supposed to have reached the amount of not less than 800,000 tons.

In 1848 it became stationary.

In 1849 many furnaces being already closed, the production of the present year can not be estimated above 650,000 tons; but from the accumulation of stock, and the difficulty of selling it, it is obvious that the diminution will be greater.

The above statement, it will be observed, is only statistical in regard to production, although it is stated that in 1821 the manufacture was in a state of ruin; and in 1842 a large portion of the furnaces were closed. This probably was in consequence of low prices that prevailed at this time.

In the report of the Secretary of the Treasury for 1863, the only official source for average prices since the war of 1812, or the panic of 1819, and prior to 1844, that I am able to obtain, is, however, sufficient for our purpose;

it is recorded that 1825, '26, and '27 were years of very high prices in pig-iron; after these years the price declined, the tariff of twelve and one-half dollars per ton was reduced in 1833, and in the year 1834 the price had declined to a very low figure for that time. Business was depressed in all branches of trade; the aggregate amount of duties on all imports were the lowest that had been collected for many years before that year; this date is forty-two years ago, and I commence my table of the ups and downs in prices of pig-iron at this time.

The finance report of 1863, in giving prices for the New York market, states that in 1836 there was a material rise in prices in all articles, especially pig-iron, which is quoted at sixty dollars per ton; and in 1837 the price advanced to seventy dollars per ton for Scotch pig, which was an extremely high price, and three years from the low prices of 1834.

The panic in money caused the suspension of specie payments by the banks in May, 1837, yet the price of pig-iron had commenced to decline in March of that year, before the panic had cast its blighting shadow over the country.

In the years 1838, '39, '40, '41, and '42 the

3

price continued to decline, and 1843 was a remarkable year for the extreme depression in prices that prevailed for all staple articles. Scotch pig was quoted in September of that year as low as twenty-two and one-half dollars per ton; this low price was six years after the high prices of 1837.

In the year 1844. the price commenced to advance, and in 1845, in the month of May, the price is quoted at fifty-two and one-half dollars per ton. The price had increased thirty dollars per ton in twenty months. The maximum price was reached in a few months less than two years from the minimum price of 1843—mark this!

Yearly average prices in Philadelphia of No. 1 Anthracite foundry pig-iron, from 1844 to 1874, both years inclusive; and production of pig-iron from 1854 to 1874 as compiled for the American Iron and Steel Association.

TABLE OF YEARLY AVERAGE PRICES.

YEAR.	PRICE.	TONS.
1844	$25\frac{3}{4}$	
1845	$29\frac{1}{4}$	
1846	$27\frac{7}{8}$	
1847	$30\frac{1}{4}$	
1848	$26\frac{1}{2}$	
1849	$22\frac{3}{4}$	
1850	$20\frac{5}{8}$	
1851	$21\frac{3}{8}$	
1852	$22\frac{5}{8}$	
1853	$36\frac{1}{2}$	
1854	$36\frac{7}{8}$	736,218.
1855	$27\frac{3}{4}$	784,178.
1856	$27\frac{1}{8}$	883,137.
1857	$26\frac{3}{8}$	798,157.
1858	$22\frac{1}{4}$	705,094.
1859	$23\frac{3}{8}$	840,627.
1860	$22\frac{3}{4}$	919,770.
1861	$20\frac{1}{4}$	731,544.
1862	$23\frac{7}{8}$	787,662.
1863	$35\frac{1}{4}$	947,604.
1864	$59\frac{1}{4}$	1,135,996.
1865	$46\frac{5}{8}$	931,582.
1866	$46\frac{7}{8}$	1,350,343.
1867	$44\frac{1}{8}$	1,461,626.
1868	$39\frac{1}{4}$	1,603,000.
1869	$40\frac{5}{8}$	1,919,641.
1870	$33\frac{1}{4}$	1,865,000.
1871	$35\frac{5}{8}$	1,912,608.
1872	$48\frac{7}{8}$	2,854,558.
1873	$42\frac{3}{4}$	2,868,278.
1874	$30\frac{1}{4}$	2,689,413.

The following are the high and low priced years in which are the highest and lowest monthly averages, which shows when the changes commence in the ups and downs of the markets for pig-iron.

In Finance Report the highest daily price in 1837, was, in January, 70 dollars per ton. In report of the Secretary Iron and Steel Association, the highest monthly averages are as follows:

1845, May,	34½ dollars per ton.	
1854, June,	38	" "
1864, August,	73⅝	" "
1872, September,	53⅞	" "

The Finance Report gives the lowest daily price for 1834, in April, 38 dollars per ton; for 1843, in July, 22½ dollars per ton.

In report of the Secretary Iron and Steel Association, the lowest monthly averages are as follows:

1850, July, ...	20 dollars per ton.	
1861, October, .	18⅝	" "
1870, December,	31¼	" "

After the high priced year 1845, the price of pig-iron declined, and in 1846, '47, '48, '49, it continued on the downward scale; and in 1850, the average by the table is 20⅞ dollars per ton, making five in number of declining

years since 1845, and recording severe depres·
sion in the iron trade, following the depressions of 1834 and 1843.

Our war with Mexico in 1846, '47, '48, and
the influx of gold from California, did not
have the effect of changing the direction of
the price of iron, as it continued to decline
during the war and after peace was declared.
After the year 1850 the price again advanced
in 1851, '52, '53 and in 1854, the price reached
the high average of 36 dollars per ton, making
four years of advances from 1850.

The uncertainty of all manufacturing business, especially the manufacture of pig-iron,
for the want of general knowledge when the
periodical decline in price is to commence—
of which it seems our sharpest and most experienced men have made mistakes, as serious
and fatal as persons of less pretensions, experience, and business qualifications—is exemplified in the following:

The *Iron King* of the Hanging Rock iron
region in Ohio, in the year 1854, was so led
astray by success and fortunate operations in
making pig-iron, as to order wood chopped
and ore mined the fall and winter of that year,
sufficient, it was claimed, to run a certain fur·
nace the succeeding year "*thirteen months out*

of twelve." As pig-iron at fifty dollars per ton
would make all furnace owners rich, it was
surely the veritable " Alladin's Lamp," and it
was only necessary for furnace men to touch
King Pig-iron and, "*mirabile dictu,*" up would
come the oriental genii with untold wealth.
But alas! what of the times? Had the chances
been studied, or were furnace men courting
the "delusive phantom of hope" and blind-
folding themselves? What did the balance
sheet of that year show? A loss of fifteen
thousand dollars. And why? Because the
price of pig-iron had tumbled in obedience to
the effects and mandates of that uniform, universal and inexorable law of over-supply and
under-demand.

  There were a host of furnace men at that
time whose thoughts were in the same chan-
nel, and who claimed that iron was the scep-
ter to wield and control the commerce of the
world; and demanded fabulous prices for their
furnace property, ignoring and forgetting the
records of past history, that iron has its ups
and downs like other articles of manufacture;
and that its power to control is as potent on
the decline as when on the advance. And in
that year 1855, without their consent and
beyond their control, and in accordance with

an established natural rule, their pig-iron was
left "high and dry," and as time glided along
in the seven succeeding years, their property
would not sell for one-half the sum that before
a reasonable price demanded. The business
became prostrated, and furnace men lost stacks
of money; the great majority of owners were
compelled to realize on their stacks of pig-iron
and sacrifice their furnace property to keep
out of bankruptcy. The price continued to
decline to the year 1861. The writer knew
of merchantable hot blast charcoal pig-iron
selling as low as thirteen dollars per ton
during the winter of 1860 and '61, in the city
of Cincinnati. The seven years from 1854 to
1861 were very disastrous to the iron trade,
and prostrated more furnaces than any period
of declines in the history of this country.

 The commercial reaction and financial difficulty of 1857, produced a general calamity;
paralyzed the hand of industry and cramped
the energies of the people for four long continued years after that revulsion.

In the fall of 1860 the banks of Baltimore,
Philadelphia, Richmond and other southern
cities suspended, and in the spring of 1861
the war of rebellion burst upon us like a clap
of thunder in a clear sky, creating terrible

disturbance in all the ramifications of business, stopping the wheels of commerce and
producing general consternation and stagnation in the iron trade.

I assert it here as a stubborn fact, as showing my faith in these cycles, that if the war
of rebellion had commenced in 1854 or in 1864,
the general course of prices for pig-iron would
have been downward in the following seven
years after 1854 and the following six years
after 1864, succeeding the same *condition to
eras* as the price after 1845 declined five years
during the Mexican war of 1846, '47 and
'48; however, the price would not have ruled
so low in 1861 and 1870 as it did in 1850. And
I also assert as an unquestionable fact, that if
we had not have had the war of rebellion from
1861 to 1865, the price of pig-iron nevertheless
would have advanced in the years 1862, '63
and '64, although the price would not have
reached so high an average as it did in these
years.

These assertions coincide with our remarks
heretofore, that war, panic, and elections do
not change the general course of prices in
their cycles; however, it may be that war and
commercial revulsions are coincident with the
advance and decline of the price of pig-iron in

the present century. Now, again we have
seen the price decline in 1865, '66, '67, '68, '69
and '70. Six years of decline, although the
averages do not run so low as they did from
1854 to 1861.

Again the price takes the ascending scale
in 1871, and scarcely two years from the minimum price of 1870 reaching the maximum in
1872, when the average of forty eight dollars
is recorded. Mark this advance, and remem-
ber the twenty months' advance from 1843 to
1845. The present cycle commencing with
the advance of 1871 and '72, and continuing
with the declines of 1873, '74 and '75, brings
us up to the present year 1876.

In the table of yearly average prices for
the year 1847, the price is higher than in
1846. The Financial Report gives the price
lower in 1847 than in 1846—there appears
this discrepancy between these two authori-
ties. Also for the year 1858 the price is
lower than in 1859; which probably was
occasioned by the panic in the fall of 1857,
depressing the price in 1858 for a short time
below its natural and proper position. And
in 1865 we also notice the price depressed a
fraction below the price of 1866. And again,
in 1868 the price is lower than in 1869. These

irregularities in the years of declines, if not
errors in compilation, are likely effects of ac-
cidental and temporary causes. In the years
of advance in the price of iron, we have none
of these irregularities.

It has been within the experience and observation of the writer; and as for himself re-
quires no authority for the information that
the price of pig-iron was very high in the
years 1837, 1845, 1854, 1864, and 1872, and
that these years were the highest priced years
since 1834; and also that the iron trade was
severely depressed in the years 1834, 1843,
1850, 1861, and 1870, and that these years were
the lowest priced years since 1834.

Now we have our data; having traveled
over the facts in a voyage of discovery and
secured our evidence, let us form our cycles
and see if we can make out a rule. Commencing with the low priced year, 1834, we
have stated that the price advanced three
years to 1837; declined six years to 1843,
making a cycle between low prices of nine
years. Again the price advanced two years to
1845, and declined five years to 1850, making
a cycle of seven years. Again advanced four
years to 1854, and declined seven years to 1861,
making a cycle of eleven years. Again ad-

vanced three years to 1864, and declined six years to 1870, making a cycle of nine years. Again advanced two years to 1872, and de· clined three years to 1875.

It will be noticed that the years of advances are as follows: 3, 2—4, 3, 2. The declines are 6, 5—7, 6, and 3, up to the present, denoting that the present declines are not full by two years, of which it is necessary to have a cycle of seven years in its order between low prices. Unless history in detail does not repeat itself, the future can not be judged by the past, and all human calculations as to cyclical movements in prices are as naught; and there is not any thing sure and certain for man at the present day and age but death and taxes.

We have so far but three years of decline from the high prices of 1872, and if the cycle of seven years, from 1843 to 1850, is to make its periodical return, and be repeated in its natural order of two years of advance and five of decline, then the cycle of seven years between low prices in its order is to be filled up from 1870 to 1877; and, therefore, we must have two years more of decline after 1875 to fill up the cycle, and we have no doubt but that "history will repeat itself" here as it has

done in other cycles which will verify and establish the accuracy of our prophecy.

Let us return to 1837, after which there are
six years of decline to 1843, and two years of
advance to 1845, making a cycle in high
prices of eight years. Again the price declines five years to 1850, and advances four
years to 1854, making a cycle of nine years.
Again the price declines seven years to 1861,
and advances three years to 1864, making a
cycle of ten years. Again declines six years
to 1870, and advances two years to 1872, making a cycle of eight years. Again declines
three years to 1875, requiring two years more
of decline, and four years of advance to make
a cycle of nine years, the next cycle in its
order, which cycle in high prices ends in the
year 1881, this year will be the next highest
priced year for pig-iron.

The following scale will enable the reader
to better understand the different cycles in
high and low prices, and the order in which
they return.

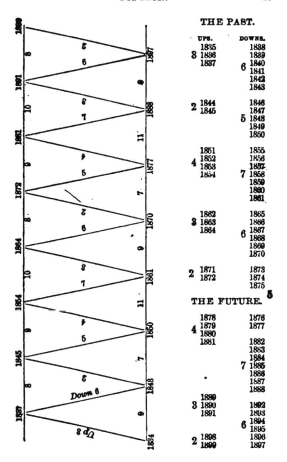

THE PAST.

UPS.	DOWNS.
1835	1838
3 1836	1839
1837	6 1840
	1841
	1842
	1843
2 1844	1846
1845	1847
	5 1848
	1849
	1850
1851	1855
1852	1856
4 1853	1857
1854	7 1858
	1859
	1860
	1861
1862	1865
3 1863	1866
1864	6 1867
	1868
	1869
	1870
2 1871	1873
1872	1874
	1875
	5

THE FUTURE.

UPS.	DOWNS.
1878	1876
4 1879	1877
1880	
1881	1882
	1883
	1884
	7 1885
.	1886
	1887
	1888
1889	
3 1890	1892
1891	1893
	1894
	6 1895
2 1898	1896
1899	1897

At the bottom of the scale is shown the lowest priced years, 1834, 1843, 1850, 1861, 1870; and in the future 1877, 1888, and 1897.

At the top are the highest priced years, 1837, 1845, 1854, 1864, and 1872; and in the future, 1881, 1891, and 1899.

This scale shows that the cycles of the lowest priced years are in a decreasing series of arithmetical progression, and in the order of 11, 9, 7, and repeat. The cycles of the highest priced years are in an increasing series of arithmetical progression, and in the order of 8, 9, 10, and repeat. Also we observe that the price of pig-iron advances and declines in a decreasing series of arithmetical progression, the advances in the order of 4, 3, and 2 years, and repeat; the declines in the order of 7, 6, and 5 years, and repeat.

Since 1834 and including 1875, the price of pig-iron has declined twenty-seven years, and advanced fourteen years, making the ratio of declines to the advances as two to one. The present cycle ending in 1877, will complete five cycles in low prices since 1834; the five cycles in high prices will be completed in 1881. The return of the commencement of the different cycles in their periodical order is twenty-seven years, one-half the ordinary life-time of man.

On page 45, the year of advances are grouped together, under the head of ups; and the years of declines under the head of downs for the old series, and continued in the future for the new series. We are now in the cycle of seven years between low priced years, and at the beginning of the fourth year of declines in this cycle, two more years will complete this cycle, and also the old series of the ups and downs.

In the year 1878 we shall enter a new series of ups and downs; the advances commencing with four years, and declines with seven years, making a cycle of eleven years in low prices. Also we are now in the cycle of nine years in high prices, and in 1881 the present high priced year cycle will be complete, and end. And after 1881 we shall enter the cycle of ten years in high prices, completing this cycle in 1891.

In the years 1878, 79, '80, and '81, the price of pig-iron will be on the ascending scale, the *iron trade will again be prosperous*, and in these years, especially the last two, 1880 and 1881, money will be made very fast in this business, unless trammeled by unwise legislation

upon the currency and tariff; and in the
year 1881, in the months of September and
October, the price will be at the highest. After
these months in that year, the price will have
a downward tendency and begin to tumble,
and it will be fortunate for all persons who
may be readers of this book, and may regu-
late their business affairs according to the
light here shown, to close out their investment at a good price in that year, and it
would be to the interest and benefit of our
whole country if our iron men, statesmen,
and others, would only take advantage of this
information, which would be the means of
placing more real money in the pockets of the
people and coffers of the nation, than the
wonderful alchemy at Washington, which is
invoked by politicians to transform old rags
into beautiful yet numberless greenbacks.

When the iron trade is depressed, so is
trade in every department of manufacture
dull and unprofitable. It is to the interests
of TRADE UNIONS to ponder and well consider
these predictions; as upon their certainty,
their losses by strikes for higher wages, or to
maintain former rates in these years of decline could be averted, by knowing the un
changeable tendencies of the times.

We have in the beginning predicted that the daily price in 1877 will run below twenty dollars per ton; and in 1881 above fifty dollars per ton. The inspiration that directs this prediction is found in the fact that "one extreme invariably follows another," and that the daily price runs below twenty dollars per ton in all the low priced years, and above fifty dollars per ton in all the high priced years.

The years 1882, '83, '84, '85, '86, '87, and '88, will be years of decline in the price of pig-iron, and years of depression in this business. These seven years of decline will be a repetition of the seven years from 1854 to 1861. We have had but one of these seven year declines since 1834, and it would be to the benefit of this country if we should never have another; however, the writer is compelled by the rule of cycles to point it out in the future, and warn the iron trade of this *impending danger*. And we proclaim it, to all who may be readers of this book, and engaged in any way in the iron trade, to be prepared after the year 1881 for breakers ahead!! What we have to say on these cycles in prices we are positive of, and we may as well, right here, state that this is a positive book.

4

In the repetition of these seven years of decline, which these cycles surely indicate, ev·
ery furnace in this country will be slaughtered,
unless backed by large capital and ability to
stand great loss, or hold their iron, stop their
furnaces, husband resources, and wait for better times, as pointed out in these pages.
These declines will not encounter a general
panic, as did the former seven year declines
in the panic of 1857, or the present five year
declines in the panic of 1873; and, therefore,
they will be more gradual.

In the years 1889, '90, and '91, the price of
pig-iron will be on the advancing scale again,
and will be three years reaching the highest
price in 1891.   This will be a period of money
making in the iron business, and these will
be three years of general prosperity in all departments of trade and industry.

After 1891 the price of pig-iron will decline
for six years, and these declines will again be
disastrous to this business; in fact, all business will be on the same retreating road to
hard pan, as they are in this year, and will be
in the next, as the iron and other trades and
industries after 1891 will be under the effects
of a commercial and financial revulsion, as
shown hereafter under the head of "Panic."

The writer now claims that his showing in the preceding pages of past prices in pig-iron, the cycles between high and low priced years, and their periodical return, has a legitimate bearing upon the future, that no one can gainsay, and no human knowledge can contradict; the predictions are based upon sound analogy; their fulfillment is demonstrated to a certainty; and that time will surely verify the prophecies.

The changes of the ups and downs in prices and cycles in the iron trade are periodical and not hap-hazard, and succeed each other in a gradual and natural order.

After the price of pig-iron has declined from the high price of fifty dollars per ton down to as low as thirty dollars per ton, the saying that then is the time to invest in the iron business, is the "*ignus fatuus*" that has swamped the iron men of this country in not having a clear conception of the number of years in which the declines continue.

We can not determine when the price of any product or commodity is at the highest or lowest by the knowledge of when prices begin to rise or fall; we can only determine that by the number of years in the ups and

downs comprising each different cycle in high
and low prices.

I will record here some axioms which must
be admitted, because they are self-evident.

That prices are high when they are above
the cost of production on a declining market.

That prices are low when they are below
the cost of production on an advancing market.

When the price of an article declines below
cost, production will diminish until demand
increases and prices advance.

When the price of an article advances
above cost, production will increase until demand ceases and prices decline.

And that the cost of production is the
wages of labor, interest on capital, and wear
of land and machinery.

When the price of pig-iron is thirty dollars
per ton, it may be either high or low, and like
a certain game with cards, the points depend
upon the trumps that are out.

If the cost of production is above on a declining market, then thirty dollars per ton is
high ; if the cost of production is below on an
advancing market, then thirty dollars per ton
is low.

The ratio of advance in price exceeds the

ratio of increase in cost of production, and there is money made very fast in the iron business during the 2, 3, and 4 years of advance in price.

On the other hand, the ratio of decline in price exceeds the ratio of decrease in the cost of production, and furnaces lose money on the 5, 6, and 7 years alternately of the decline in price, unless wages and expenses are curtailed in time.

To apply our CAST IRON RULE, when the price of pig-iron has been as high as fifty dollars per ton, the price in the succeeding years has invariably declined to twenty dollars per ton ; and, *vice versa*, when the price has been as low as twenty dollars per ton, the price afterward, in a certain number of years, has advanced as high as fifty dollars per ton.

The iron business is a very uncertain trade for persons to engage in who are not acquainted with the number of years in which the price advances, as they are only from two to four years, while the declines are from five to seven years.

The enormous home production and excessive importation of foreign iron in 1871 and 1872 produced a break in prices, and with the over production of 1873 and 1874, and the

panic of 1873, the iron trade is again prostrated.

To persons not acquainted with the rules
by which these changes occur, as regulated by
an overruling providence, it is to them a
wonderful illustration of the peculiarities of
trade and the uncertainty of prices, as attempted to be explained by our limited
knowledge of supply and demand.

In the spring of 1872 the country was prosperous and advancing beyond all past history; railroads were extending their lines
across the continent in every direction, mark-
ing the most gigantic railroad expansion the
world ever beheld; creating an unprecedented demand for iron, giving an impetus to the
manufacture thereof, that had no parallel in
the history of this or any other country, running the production to nearly three millions
of tons in that year. All at once comes a
snap and a crash: a reaction sets in so speedy
and terrible, so general and decided, that we
become amazed at the mysterious workings
of this trade and the decrees of an all-wise
Providence.

The decline in the price of pig-iron since
1872 has been over fifty per cent.

Iron masters are crying out, "Give us protection or we are ruined," while the silent whisper to "reduce the product" is not willingly and generally heard. The Secretary of the Iron and Steel Association reports that out of 701 furnaces on the first of February, 1874, there were 398 stacks out of blast; nevertheless there were fifty new furnaces completed in 1873, thirty-eight in 1874, and forty-six stacks in the course of erection, and other new furnaces projected in 1875. What blindness and what folly ! !

The remedy at present is not to be found in a tariff alone on foreign importation; a home competition is here in our midst more formidable than all foreign competition combined. SEVEN HUNDRED FURNACES, some of which cast *one hundred tons of metal per day*, are ready to swell the home production on the first show of an advance in price, beyond the most extraordinary consumption, and producing stagnation more disastrous than ever.

It is a hard alternative for furnace men to be compelled by the "logic of facts and events," to blow out their furnaces and suspend business for so long a time, but to be " forewarned is to be forearmed ;" is it not the part of wisdom and policy to stop before the capital is gone and stock unprofitably consumed ?

We have not seen, in our experience or observation, neither do the facts and records of
modern history show, a permanent advance
until after five years from the highest price ;
and is the present decline and cycle to be an
exception to all others? and in the face of,
and succeeding the greatest supplying capacity the world has ever witnessed ? and when
other manufactures and trades, and all rail-
roading is depressed and unprofitable, and
when all Europe stands ready to supply any
demand at pauper prices outside of · this
country ?

VERILY, the hand-writing is upon the wall,
and so plain it needs no magi to decipher
what it means.

HOGS.

The history of the HOG CROP and its various manufactures and products is intimately
connected with the growth and progress of
the CORN CROP, and the price of one now
generally fluctuates with the price of the
other.

The packing of pork before the era of railroads was confined to very narrow limits, and
there was not much value placed upon the
hog at that period, as will be seen by the fol-

lowing sketch written by Charles Cist, of
Cincinnati, Ohio:

"Hog raising has always been a profitable,
and therefore a favorite department of farming in what was formerly called the West,
but which now constitutes the great center, as
respects population, of our rapidly expanding
republic. The rich harvests, to be had simply for the gathering, yielded by the oak,
beech, hickory, and other trees of our forests,
popularly termed mast, formed, to a great extent, for many years, fattening food for swine.
The roots in the woods, with the natural
grasses, supplied subsistence during the spring
and summer months, so that the sole expense
to the farmer, in raising hogs, was the feeding
of those too young for market, and of those
reserved for stock and for increase, at the cost
of the Indian corn necessary for their winter
sustenance. In early days, and before the introduction of railways, this cereal would not
repay the expense of transportation to market, and therefore hardly entered into the con-
sideration of what it cost to raise hogs. In
fact, taking into view the prolific character
of the animal, and the small amount of labor
and expense involved in its care and cure, it
was the general impression in the West that it

cost nothing for a man to make his own pork,
and for a long time vast quantities of slaughtered hogs were sold in this region at prices
ranging from seventy-five cents to one dollar
per hundred weight, and considered suffi-
ciently remunerative at these rates. The
writer has seen in the southern portion of
Illinois, and within twenty-five miles of land
carriage to the Ohio, immense quanties of
Indian corn offered at six cents per bushel;
yet at this low figure the grain would not
bear transportation to the river.

"The farmer, unless in the neighborhood of
a distillery, was compelled to feed his crop to
his cattle or hogs. Even at a much later
date, between the scarcity of timber for fuel,
and the low price of corn, large quantities of
the latter article have furnished fuel in the
prairie region of the State referred to.

"As the cultivation of the country opened
and the wood ranges became more restricted,
it was found that it paid better, while it was
more convenient, to feed the hogs on corn than
to turn them out to the woods, as they grew
faster and increased more rapidly in fat as
well as in flesh, while the quality both of
meat and lard, was thereby greatly enhanced
in value. At this period, for want of good

roads, grain to a limited extent only was sold
to the whisky distillers; its low price not
permitting it to be carried by wagons to the
distilleries unless from short distances. Under
these circumstances pork packers commenced
at various points in the West for the supply
of the eastern markets, while the rapid increase of hogs kept pace with the correspond-
ing improvement of the western country and
the enlargement of its corn crops.

"Then came the era of railroads. It was at
once seen that hogs could be delivered at
market points, either East or West, at less
expense, in shorter time and in better condition, than they had hitherto been taken by
droves. There was also no giving out of the
hogs on the route. The natural result was to
give a new impulse to the raising of swine;
and from that period the hog became one of
the most important staples of the country."

In examining the history of prices for hogs
the past half century, we find that the price
ruled very low up to the year 1830. This was
the period when there was so little demand
in Cincinnati for any portion of the hog other
than hams, shoulders, sides and lard, that the
heads, spare ribs, neck pieces, back bones, etc.,
were regularly thrown into the Ohio river to

get rid of them. Afterwards, in 1835 the products of the hog became more valuable, and in the year 1836, in the city of New York, the price of mess pork advanced to thirty dollars per barrel, and lard to eighteen cents per pound. (See Finance Report of 1863.) This year was a very high priced year for hogs and their product. I have not been able to get the average price for fat hogs at this time, as there were probably none compiled; therefore we are compelled to take the price of product as we find it given by official authority. After the year 1836 the price of product declined each year to 1842. Mess pork was quoted in New York at six dollars and seventy-five cents per barrel. The highest quotation in the decade from 1840 to 1850, was in the year 1847, the great famine year in Ireland. Mess pork in New York City was sixteen dollars per barrel, eleven years from the high prices of 1836. Mark this!

I have not been able to collect reliable yearly average prices for fat hogs prior to the year 1855, as there appears to be no sources accessible to obtain them; and as I have not the evidence to show any noticeable periodicity or regularity existing in the return of *low prices* before that time, I therefore commence my table of averages in the year 1855, which is twenty-one years ago, and forty years since 1836, the commencement of our cycles in high prices for product and hogs.

Table of average prices for fat hogs at Cincinnati, Ohio, since 1855, and the whole number of hogs packed in the West during the winter seasons of 1849, '50 to 1874, '75, inclusive, as compiled by the *Cincinnati Price Current.*

YEARS.	NO. OF HOGS.	PRICE NET.	GROSS.
1849	1,652,220		
1850	1,332,867		
1851	1,182,846		
1852	2,201,110		
1853	2,534,770		
1854	2,124,404		
1855	2,489,502	$6.05	$4.84
1856	1,818,468	6.23	4.99
1857	2,210,778	5.16	4.13
1858	2,405,552	6.58	5.27
1859	2,350,822	6.21	4.97
1860	2,155,702	5.97	4.78
1861	2,893,666	3.28	2.63
1862	4,069,520	4.45	3.56
1863	3,261,105	7.00	5.60
1864	2,422,779	14.62	11.70
1865	1,785,955	11.96	9.57
1866	2,490,791	7.52	6.02
1867	2,781,084	8.25	6.60
1868	2,499,873	10.51	8.41
1869	2,635,312	11.82	9.46

YEARS.	NO. OF HOGS.	PRICE NET.	GROSS.
1870	3,695,251	$8.25	$6.60
1871	4,831,558	5.45	4.36
1872	5,410,314	4.90	3.92
1873	5,466,200	5.73	4.58
1874	5,566,226	8.74	6.99

Average price at Cincinnati for 20 years is $7.43 net or $5.94 gross.

The difference that Cincinnati pays above the average for the West is as follows:

	1872	1873	1874
Cincin'ti net.	$4.90	$5.73	$8.74
West "	4.65	5.43	8.33
	25	30	41

These dates refer to the years in which the crop was made. The packing season commences in November and ends in the following March. It is shown in the table that the average price for hogs was greater in 1856 than in 1855, but less in 1857. This depression in the advance was produced by the panic, however, in 1858, the general course of price asserts itself with an average higher than either of the three years preceding it. After the high priced year 1858, the average starts out on the descending scale, declines in 1859, '60 and '61, making three years of declines with an average in 1861 of two dollars and

sixty three cents per hundred weight gross.
This year was the beginning of the war, when
farmers were almost compelled to give away
their hogs on account of the low prices that
prevailed.

It is a well known fact to the farmers and
packers, that when the price of hogs advanced
in 1862, '63 and '64, that all parties made
money; and that these years of advances culminated in 1864 with an average of eleven
dollars and seventy cents per hundred
weight gross, which is the highest yearly
average price ever paid in this country for
hogs. In the years 1865 and '66, the average
price declines, making only two years of decline after 1864. In 1867 the price takes the
ascending scale,—higher in 1868, and still
higher in 1869, with an average of nine dollars
and forty six cents per hundred weight gross,
making three years of advance after 1866.
After the year 1869 the price took the descending scale; lower in 1870, '71 and '72, getting
down to the average of three dollars and ninety
cents per hundred weight gross, making three
years of decline after 1869. In the year 1873
the price advanced notwithstanding the great
revulsion in trade of that year, and continued
to advance in 1874; and the average will be

higner in 1875 than in 1874, making three
years of advances since 1872.

Now let us go back in review and form our
cycles. Commencing with 1836, a high priced
year in product, we find the next high priced
year in product to be the year 1847, eleven
years from 1836. Extending this eleven years
forward we have the high priced year 1858;
our commencing year in high average prices
for hogs. Extending the time eleven years
further gives us the high priced year 1869,
making three eleven year cycles in high
prices.

Again let us return to the year 1850, a low
priced year for hogs, and add eleven to that
year, and we have the year 1861 a low priced
year; add eleven again, anâ we have 1872, a
low priced year, making three eleven-year
cycles in low prices.

But we are traveling too fast, and we must
return to 1847, a high-priced year. After this
year the price declined three years to 1850,
and then advanced three years to 1853, making a shorter cycle of six years in high prices;
also after 1853 the price declined two years to
1855, and then advanced three years to 1858,
making a cycle of five years in high prices,
and these two shorter cycles from 1847 to

1858, making an eleven year cycle. After
1858 the price declined three years to 1861,
and then advanced three years to 1864, making a short cycle of six years in high prices.
Also after 1864 the price declined two years to
1866, and afterwards advanced three years to
1869, making a cycle of five years in high
prices, and completing another long cycle of
eleven years. Now, again, after 1869 the price
declined three years to 1872, and then advanced three years to 1875, making a cycle
again of six years in high prices, and completing one of the short cycles composing the
present eleven year cycle, which will end
with a short cycle of five years in the year
1880. Returning to 1850, the next low priced
year was 1855, making a cycle of five years in
low prices. After 1855 the next low priced
year was 1861, making a cycle of six years in
low prices. Again after 1861 the next low-
priced year was 1866, making a cycle of five
years in low prices. After 1866 the following
low priced year was 1872, making a cycle of
six years in low prices.

It will be noticed that the short cycles composing the eleven year cycles in high prices,
since 1847, have been alternately six and five
years; and the short cycles in low prices, since
5

1850, have been alternately five and six years.

The axiom, "History repeats itself," implies a cyclical movement in human affairs, and as it is a generally received opinion that every thing moves in cycles, especially in nature, we are forced to predict, judging the future by the past, that in the years 1876 and '77 the price of hogs must decline in the average, so as to fill the required number of years necessary to complete the present five and eleven year cycles in low prices ending in 1877; also after two years of decline there must be three years of advances to the year 1880, to complete the next five and eleven year cycles in high prices, and therefore demonstrating to a certainty and to the comprehension of all, the fulfillment of our second series of prophecies.

On the following page is a scale of years to enable the reader to see the different cycles in their order, also the ups and downs in prices for the past and in the future.

This scale shows the years of lowest and highest prices for the hog and its products since 1836, coming down in five and six year cycles after 1847. At the top of the scale are the highest priced years, 1836, 1847, 1853, 1858, 1864, 1869, and 1875 for the past, and

PAST.

UPS.	DOWNS.
1856	1859
1857	1860
1858	1861
1862	
1863	1865
1864	1866
1867	1870
1868	1871
1869	1872
1873	
1874	
1875	

FUTURE.

UPS.	DOWNS.
1878	1876
1879	1877
1880	
1884	1881
1885	1882
1886	1883
1889	
1890	1887
1891	1888

1880, 1886, and 1891 for the future. At the bottom are the lowest priced years, 1850, 1855, 1861, 1866, 1872, for the past, and 1877, 1883, and 1888 for the future.

We have now passed out of the cycle of six years in high prices, the year 1875 closing this cycle. The next cycle in high prices will require five years ending in 1880; at that time the price of hogs will be high.

We are also in the cycle of five years in low prices, this cycle ending in 1877, when the price of hogs will be low, and farmers complaining about the prices they are compelled to accept for their hogs. Pig-iron will also be at a low price at that time, placing agriculture and manufacture at a low ebb; prices low all round will make "hard times" and "dull trade."

After 1877 agriculture and manufacture will go hand in hand, the price of hogs and pig-iron will be on the ascending scale, business in all departments will improve up to the year 1880 and 1881, after that time prices will decline and advance alternately in each different branch of trade, until the year 1891, when general business will culminate throughout the country, especially with iron and hogs, two of the most important and leading branches of trade.

It is to be observed that the price of hogs do not go up and down with the number of hogs packed. By referring to the column in 1858, a high priced year, the packing exceeds any previous year with the exception of 1853. In 1862 the price advanced with the enormous packing of four millions of hogs. In 1869 the price advanced, while the packing exceeded that of 1868; and also the same may be said of 1873 and 1874 over the packing of 1872.

The price of hogs invariably advance three years in succession. In the year 1859 the price declined, while the packing was short of 1858. Also in 1860 the price declined, while the packing was short of 1859. In 1865 the price declined, while the packing was short of 1864 600,000 hogs.

In some of the years, as the packing increased or decreased in number, so the price advanced or declined; an increase of packing diminished the price, and *vice versa*. Therefore it is not safe to rely too much upon results based upon the number of hogs packed.

The price of hogs decline two and three years alternately in the cycles of low priced years.

The aggregate number of hogs in all **the**
states and territories, as estimated by the Department of Agriculture at Washington in
1873, was 32,632,000; in 1874, was 30,860,900.
The packing in 1873 and 1874 was about one-
sixth of the whole number in each year.
Chicago packs more pork than any city in the
United States or in Europe. Total number
packed in 1874 was 1,690,348 hogs—nearly
one-third of the whole packing of 1874.

As the winter packing of hogs is only about
one-sixth of the total number produced, it is
an important question what becomes of the
other five-sixths, and what proportion is annually killed. I must acknowledge this to be
a task, to undertake to make out such an account by any system outside of the art of
"double-entry book-keeping." Almost every
farmer's family, for domestic consumption, kill
from one to twenty or more hogs every year,
and there has never been any statistics compiled for a record of the number thus slaughtered.

There were engaged in farming, according
to the census of 1870, 5,922,471 persons, about
one-sixth of the population; if each farmer had
killed on the average but one hog, the aggregate would exceed the total winter packing for

commerce of 1874. Then we must consider the number of hogs that have been slaughtered by butchers in the cities and towns, the number that annually die with disease, and also the number that is reserved for stock and for increase. From these facts we can understand why the price is not altogether governed by the number of hogs packed in our large cities; since 1868 the number of hogs packed has yearly increased.

Every farmer, feeder, drover, and packer, should know the years in which the price of hogs are to advance or decline. There are seldom any two years in succession in which the average price ranges the same. In the table of averages, there are two years in which they are the same, 1867 and 1870; however, they are three years apart, one on the advance, the other on the decline.

In the years 1858, 1864, and 1869, a great many persons made money on hogs, and, elated with good fortune, were tempted to try again in 1859, 1865, and 1870; and through ignorance of the workings of the ups and downs in prices, were caught with one dollar corn-fed into six dollar hogs, and they lost the profits and gains of the preceding years, and no doubt the same will be repeated by

others in 1876; as 1875 was a profitable and
a high priced year. We see continually some
of our best traders "caught out in the wet,"
and to some persons it will always require a
Columbus to show them how the egg is to
stand upon its end.

The price that hogs will bring each year
can be approximated by the course of the past
averages; however, it is governed by supply
and demand, and state of trade in reference
to the past commercial revulsion and the future coming crisis and the condition of the
currency. Periodical revulsions do not in
their effects change the general course of
prices in their cycles, but they have a temporary influence to depress prices below their
natural and proper position, and an after influence to keep down the averages to lower
limits. If the people would only learn such
years and stay out of this business, or confine
themselves to smaller trade, when these declines in prices are to take place, especially
after panic years, they would not complain so
much of "hard times" and "high taxes."

Farmers think that packers do not pay a
sufficient price for hogs, when prices are on
the decline.

Packers think they are paying too much for hogs, when prices are on the advance.

Now in both cases, *farmers and packers* are at a loss to know what the future development of prices will be.

In the farmer's case, he receives all there is in the market, whether it covers cost or not, and the packer loses money on the further decline.

In the packer's case, he pays the market price, and makes money on the further advance.

It is an established fact that the quantity of hogs in this country is ruled and governed by the current price of corn.

In the commencement of the periodical advance in the price of corn, and until it reaches the highest price, large shoats are marketed and butchered, the hogs that should be wintered are slaughtered; small farmers and feeders sell their stock hogs in the fall and winter, to large feeders and speculators. In consequence of hogs being massed they get overlaid by large numbers bedding together during the cold and inclemency of the winter; and without the use of the kitchen-slops, and by the use of soft, frosted, and rotten corn, peculiar to these years, they become diseased, and therefore more die by cholera, thumps, and other diseases.

On the other hand when the price of corn begins its periodical decline, and until it gets to the lowest, farmers and small feeders keep their stock hogs, and by the more equal distribution in smaller numbers, hogs live, are more healthy and plenty. Farmers think it will pay better to feed their corn to stock hogs, and raise more young hogs, than to sell their corn on a declining market; but in this they are mistaken, as they are unknowingly producing cheap pork for the whole world, by an over production, the surplus of which has to go out of the country for consumers.

The amount of hog products exported corresponds inversely with the prices; whenever we export large amounts they are at low prices, and when prices are high our exports are inconsiderable.

To sell corn and hogs at the market price in the fall to others who have not studied the chances, the production in the years of decline is made profitable by them who know when to come in out of the storm. When the periodical advance in the price of hogs is approaching, the butchers, drovers, and packers secure contracts by subtle arguments with the

farmers for their hogs, and as a consequence
the farmers are not benefited to the full extent of the advance, as they are induced to
engage too soon, therefore they lose the opportunities which belong to them. It is the
usual expression and opinion that when a
farmer has his hogs fat, that then is the time
to sell; this depends upon what cycle of seasons and prices are ruling in the markets of
our country. If on the periodical decline,
after a year of short crops and high prices
the previous year, such as 1858, '64, '69, and
'75, then would be the time to sell. If on the
periodical advance after a year of good crops
and low prices the previous year, such as 1861,
'66, and 72, then if you have a little "speculation in your eye," it no doubt would be a good
time, and pay you to hold for a rise.

As buyers and sellers of products we can
only be gainers by scarcity and high prices,
and that only for that article which was obtained when plenty and at low prices.

Speculating in hogs is generally with the
majority a matter of *heads and tails;* when
successful they are owlish wise, and of course
know all about it; but when tails, then the
"devil is in the *hog.*" It is a most signifi-
cant fact in these price cycles, and a confirma-

tion of the theory that _God is in prices_—that
the price of corn and hogs could advance in
the years 1873, '74, and '75, during and immediately succeeding the great revulsion in
trade of 1873, and when all business was be-
coming depressed and prostrated in manufacturing industry, trade unions striking to
maintain former rates, mills and furnaces
closing their doors, merchants complaining of
dull times, millions of laborers and mechanics
idle, and no work to do. Yet we say, notwithstanding all this, corn, hogs, and provisions
have advanced in price in these years; for the
cycle of six years in high prices from 1869 to
1875 was to be filled, and it would have been
contrary to the order and laws of nature to
have been otherwise.

CORN.

This cereal is known as the largest of all the
grain crops, and one of the most useful products known to man. It is the chief basis for
provisions, and a very important element in
our breadstuff supplies. Notwithstanding the
greater value of wheat per bushel, corn is the
great item in the prosperity of the West, and
upon the good price of corn depends the wel-
fare of the farmer. A large and over-estimated

corn crop, that reduces the price to a nominal
sum, makes farmers feel poor, and in turn re-
acts upon merchants and manufacturers, and
brings about dull trade.

Our agricultural products and stock are the
basis and support of all commerce, and of all
business and trade in every department of
human activity, and upon which all other
industries rest. Their scarcity or abundance
depends upon the seasons, and mostly require
a year to bring them to perfection and ma-
turity, while manufactured commodities can
generally be produced in any quantity, and
in a much shorter time.

The commerce of the world is so dependent
upon agricultural productions, that to ascertain their probable annual amount, has become an object of the greatest utility. A
scarcity or abundance of crops affects the ex-
changes of the world, and tends to forecast
future prices, and to give some clue to future
production.

Estimated yield of corn in the United
States from 1840 to 1874—the years 1862,
'63, and '64, for Northern States only—and
average prices from 1862 to 1874 inclusive,
collected from agricultural and statistical reports.

YEARS.	PRODUCTION.	AVERAGE PRICES. CTS.
1840 . . .	377,000,000 . . .	
1850 . . .	592,000,000 . . .	
1860 . . .	838,000,000 . . .	
1862 . . .	533,000,000 . . .	34
1863 . . .	397,000,000 . . .	69
1864 . . .	530,000,000 . . .	99
1865 . . .	704,000,000 . . .	46
1866 . . .	867,000,000 . . .	68
1867 . . .	768,000,000 . . .	69
1868 . . .	906,000,000 . . .	62
1869 . . .	774,000,000 . . .	75
1870 . . .	1,094,000,000 . . .	54
1871 . . .	991,000,000 . . .	48
1872 . . .	1,092,000,000 . . .	39
1873 . . .	932,000,000 . . .	48
1874 . . .	854,000,000 . . .	65

If we could have yearly average prices of
corn for the whole country since 1825, we
would find that they would show the same
regularity in ups and downs that they do after
1862. The Finance Report of 1863 in giving
prices for the New York markets (which are
a long ways from the corn producing states)
shows that prices were very high in 1825, '26,
in 1836, '37, in 1847 and in 1858. The statistics of the Department of Agriculture show that
the average price was very high for 1864; in
fact higher than ever before in this country;
and again the price is at the top figures in

1869, as can be seen in the table of yearly average prices for corn. The average price for 1875 will be high, and it is the next high priced year after 1869. These high priced years correspond with the price of hogs. These years are the highest priced years since 1830, making eleven year cycles up to 1858, afterwards in short cycles of 6 and 5 years to 1864, '69 and '75. The next high priced year for corn, which is in the future, will be the year 1880, eleven years from 1869, and five years from 1875.

We find the cycles of eleven years in low prices by taking the quotations in the Finance Report of 1863 for the New York markets, and commencing in 1828, a low priced year, running to 1840, then to 1850, and to 1861; afterwards according to the yearly averages, as shown in our table to 1872, the last low priced year. The next low priced year coming down to five year cycles, will be in 1877, and the one following eleven years from 1872, will be 1883.

The same scale of prices for hogs will answer for corn. When the price of hogs has been high the price of corn has been high, and the same when the price of hogs has been low, the price of corn has been correspondingly low. After 1858, high and low priced years run in

the same order of six and five year cycles in
the price of corn that they do for hogs.

Now judging the future by the past, and
looking to history to repeat itself with approximate accuracy in detail, it is our judg-
ment upon which we predicate this prophecy,
that the average price of corn up to the year
1891, will advance and decline with the average price of hogs, as shown in the scale of
cycles in the price of hogs; and that the general advance and decline in the price of corn,
will precede the general advance and decline
in the price of hogs. This is inferred from
the fact, as before stated, that the current price
of corn governs the quantity of hogs in this
country.

The price of hogs, if $2.50 gross, on the
farm, will realize to the farmer 25 cents per
bushel for his corn.

$3.00	Gross,	30 cents per Bushel.
4.00	"	40 " " "
5.00	"	50 " " "
6.00	"	60 " " "
7.00	"	70 " " "
8.00	"	80 " " "
9.00	"	90 " " "
10.00	"	100 " " "

The average prices gross for hogs compared

with the average prices for corn per bushel since 1862, in which the fact can be noticed that the price of one follows the price of the other in the ups and downs since the year 1868 as regularly as evening follows morning.

	HOGS, GROSS.	CORN PER BUSHEL.
1862 . .	3.56	34c.
1863 . .	5.60	69
1864 . .	11.70	99
1865 . .	9.57	46
1866 . .	6.02	68
1867 . .	6.60	69
1868 . .	8.41	62
1869 . .	9.46	75
1870 . .	6.60	54
1871 . .	4.36	48
1872 . .	3.92	39
1873 . .	4.58	48
1874 . .	6.99	65
1875 . .		

Average prices for 1875 not collected and published in time for this book.

The corn crop never falls short in the growing corn as much as one-half, but a large crop can be cut short by frosts, floods, damp, etc., in the amount secured. It is not so much in the failure of the crop, as in that which is done with it.

The rational explanation of the partial
6

failure of the corn crop in any one year, may be found in the peculiarities of the seasons. The number of acres planted is no criterion of future production and prices.

We were well informed in the summer of 1874, by the Agricultural Bureau at Washington, the commercial bulletins of the East, and crop reporters of the West, that there were two million more acres in corn that year than in the year 1873. Some of the eastern papers were clamorous that the crops of 1874 were simply enormous, and that prices would rule very low; therefore the "bears" of the East commenced to fix the price of corn on the supposition of very great abundance, while the merchants began to grow concerned about their stocks of merchandise, for fear the farmers in their poverty would not be able to take the usual amount. Now what was the corn crop and price for 1874, compared with 1873, taking the estimates of the Department of Agriculture for production and prices, as they are the only statistics at my command.

1873,	Production,	932,000,000	Price,	48c.
1874.	"	854,000,000	"	65c.
		78,000,000		17c.

A decrease of seventy-eight million of bushels in product, and an increase of seventeen cents in price.

This surely shows if there can be any dependence placed upon these statistics, that seasons make large or small crops, and that future prices can not be foretold by the acreage planted or sown.

The number of acres in corn and production in all the states and territories in the year

1872	was	35,526,836	product	1,092,000,000
1873	"	39,197,148	"	932,000,000
		3,670,312		160,000,000

This statement shows an increase in area planted of three million six hundred and seventy thousand three hundred and twelve acres, while there was a decrease in product of one hundred and sixty million of bushels, with an advance in average price in 1873 over 1872 of nine cents per bushel.

This increase in area planted is equal to the whole number of acres in corn in 1873 in the great state of Iowa, the second state in the union for corn. With this very large addition in area for corn, it is a surprising fact

that the number of bushels produced was one
hundred and sixty million of bushels less
than the year before.

Is it any wonder that some operate upon an
overestimate, and others on an underestimate,
when we see that the seasons have so much
influence to make large or small crops, and
also when our knowledge is so limited in regard to meteorological phenomena, which repeat themselves in well defined and established periods?

It has been argued, and is proverbial, that it
does not make any difference to the farmers
whether they raise large or small crops in the
aggregate; what they lose in price they gain
in quantity, and what they lose in quantity
they gain in price.

Now let us see if statistics of agriculture
will carry out this assertion. Let us take the
last cycle of six years between high prices of
which we have the yearly average prices, for
all the states and territories. Commencing
with the high priced year 1869, and ending
in 1874, the year before the next high priced
year, giving us three years of small production and high prices, and three years of large
production and low prices.

Years in which were the smallest number
of bushels produced and highest prices:

1869	774,000,000	75c.	58,050,000
1873	932,000,000	48c.	44,731,000
1874	854,000,000	65c.	55,510,000
	2,560,000,000	.	158,296,000

Years in which were the largest number
of bushels produced and lowest prices:

1870	1,094,000,000	54c.	59,076,000
1871	991,000,000	48c.	47,568,000
1872	1,092,000,000	39c.	42,588,000
	3,177,000,000		149,232,000

In the large crop years of 1870, '71, and '72,
there was produced six hundred and seventeen millions of bushels more of corn than in
the small crop years of 1869, '73, and '74, and
there was realized in these small crop years
by the farmers, nine million and sixty-four
thousand dollars more money.

This statement is as clear to the world as
the light from a *kerosene* lamp, if there can be
any approximate correctness in the estimates
of the Department of Agriculture, that it
does make a difference, and that all the labor
employed and exerted, and expenses incurred

to produce and handle this six hundred and
seventeen millions of bushels more of corn in
1870, '71, and '72, than in 1869, '73, and '74,
was so much labor and money literally thrown
away so far as the farmers' direct gains were
concerned, while they should have raised
twenty millions of bushels more corn to have
realized the same money that was realized
out of these short crop years.

Let us make a comparison by taking the
years in this cycle of the greatest extremes
in production:

1869	. . 774,000,000	75c.	58,050,000
1872	. . 1,092,000,000	39c.	42,588,000
	318,000,000		15,462,000

There were produced in 1872 three hundred
and eighteen millions of bushels more of corn
than in 1869, and there were realized fifteen
million four hundred and sixty-two thousand
dollars less money.

As corn was cheap in 1872, and the farmers
fed a great portion of it to hogs, let us see
how they came out with hogs:

1869 .	2,635,312	hogs packed	9.46,	24,930,051
1872 .	5,410,314	" "	3.92,	21,208,430
	2,775,002			3,721,621

In 1872 there was sold to packers two mil
lion seven hundred and seventy-five thousand
and two hogs more in 1872 than in 1869, and
the farmers realized three million seven hundred and twenty-one thousand six hundred
and twenty-one dollars less money.

It is evident that in the years of decline to
lower prices, a large over-estimated yield is
not the boon desired by the farmer, and it is
undoubtedly to the interest of the farmer to
use more of that energy that relaxes no effort;
the perseverance that never grows weary in
'striving to produce more corn in the years of
advances towards higher prices.

The farmer, however, is placed in the same
category in respect to low prices that the manufacturer is placed; if the farmer has to take
a low price for his grain and stock at intervals, he is compensated in being enabled to
purchase manufactured commodities in their
low priced years, therefore alternately each
has its years of high and low prices that
either can take advantage of.

It is to the interest of the farmer not to be
governed too much by present demand, and
not to continue in the course it directs too
long. The demand can be calculated—the
population does not always vary with the

seasons; it is the supply that makes generally the fluctuations in prices. It is in the
nature of things that the farmer should receive the benefit of three years advance in his
corn and hogs in every cycle of prices, and it
would be injustice to him if he should be
compelled to lose his labor and toil by the
wolfish and bearish cry of enormous crops and
low prices.

The ups and downs in prices for corn, hogs,
and pig-iron, and the activity and depression
in general trade, are no doubt caused by an
over and under production for a term of years,
and the writer has an idea that these cycles
in prices, which are so well defined, and repeat themselves with such surprising accuracy, are connected in some way with the
cycles of nature, which are fixed because they
are produced by regularly and permanently
fixed causes, which are constant and uniform.

The peculiarities of the weather and atmospheric currents, producing these extremes
which are not conducive to large crops of
either stock or grain, were seen in the polar
current which came down from high latitudes on a course parallel to the Rocky Moun-
tains in the year of 1874, producing the sever-
est and most continued cold we have exper-

ienced for eleven years, since the winter of
1863–'64, and in the summer of 1875 the trop.
ical current or trade winds being deflected by
the Mexican elevations, entered the great
basin of the Mississippi, and again deflected
by the mountain spurs in Alabama, they
swept freely over the states of Kentucky,
Ohio, Indiana, Illinois, Missouri, and Iowa;
the great corn region of the world, laden with
the aqueous vapors of the Gulf of Mexico,
and coming in contact and condensed by these
cold northern currents, occasioned in June,
July, and August of 1875 the greatest amount
of rain-fall and most disastrous floods since the
years 1836, 1847, and 1858.

In all the years prior to and including the
high priced years in corn and hogs, we have
had extremes in the weather. We had
droughts in 1845, '46, and heavy rain-falls in
1847. The heat droughts and cold winters of
1856, '57, and '58 were very remarkable. The
cold winters and droughts of 1863, '64, were
unprecedented. Extremes of heat, rain, and
droughts in 1868 and '69 were disastrous to
the crops, and the same can be said of 1873,
'74, and '75. The years 1879 and 1880 will
again be years of extremes in the weather,
producing short crops and high prices.

We have the information from high astronomical authority, that in the year 1880 we are
to have a planetary combination as to three
of the largest planets connected with our solar
system, such as has not occurred before for
about 2,300 years. These planets are all to
reach the nearest point in their orbits to the
sun at the same time, having the effect upon
the earth of the most violent and wonderful
changes in her atmospheric and magnetic
system that has ever been recorded in history.

COTTON.

To give contemporary testimony to corrob-
orate and verify our price cycles in corn and
hogs, we will take the price of cotton, which
grows out from the ground, and is affected by
the weather. Corn and cotton occupy all the
territory lying between the lakes and gulf.
The cotton crop of the Mississippi would be
affected by the floods at the North whenever
we would have extraordinary rain-falls, or by
unusual early or late frosts.

The price of cotton collected from Finance
Reports of 1857, '58, '63, and '73, these prices
being from the most reliable sources accessible in the absence of any other official record:

1821	16c.		1855		8c.	
1822	16		1856		9	
1823	11		1857		12	
1824	15		1858		11	
1825	20		1859		11	
1826	12		1860		10½	
1827	10		1861		16	
1828	10		1862		41	
1829	10		1863		74	
1830	9		1864	1	05	11
1831	9	11	1865		57	
1832	9		1866		40	
1833	11		1867		23	
1834	12		1868		26	
1835	16		1869		29	
1836	16		1870		20	
1837	14		1871		17	
1838	10		1872		22	
1839	14		1873		19	
1840	8		1874			
1841	10		1875			11
1842	8	11	1876			
1843	6		1877			
1844	8		1878			
1845	5		1879			
1846	7		1880			
1847	10					
1848	7					
1849	6					11
1850	11					
1851	12					
1852	8	11				
1853	9					
1854	9		1891			

These prices are for New York, which are sometimes ruled by speculators, and allowance must be made for their incorrectness.

The price of cotton is more influenced by the state of trade in the world than the price of corn and hogs, and therefore it does not follow the production in this country so close as the former products. Commencing in 1825, we find the price of cotton to be twenty cents per pound, the highest quotation in the scale —except during the war of rebellion; the next highest quotation is in 1836, eleven years from 1825. In looking ahead in the table, we find 1847 a high priced year in respect to other years preceding and immediately after that year. Again in 1858, we find a high price with the year before and the year after, all high priced years. Again, in 1869 we have the next high price after the war, the war coming in on a short cycle of six years. Now extending our price cycle of eleven years from 1869, it gives us the year 1880, our next high priced year for cotton, and running eleven years further, we have the year 1891, when cotton, corn, hogs, pig-iron, will be at a high price, and general business prosperous—up to that year.

PROVISIONS.

The year of the provision trade begins the first of November and ends on the last day of October.

The statistics are mostly made up commencing with November. However, with these statistics, as generally compiled, the writer in his observation does not lay much store by them.

How many hogs are annually killed is one of the mooted and unsolved problems of the day. The statistics of winter and summer packing of hogs are no doubt reliable, or as near correct as can be compiled, but the domestic killing by farmers and butchers is not collated for the public, which is a very important item to be considered in our provision statistics. Therefore we are forced to take for granted that a part is not sufficient without the whole.

It is almost an impossibility to procure full and reliable statistics of the exact amount of hog products in this country; and also what becomes of all the pork, bacon, lard, etc., that are prepared in this country to be consumed at home, or sold to commerce. And again, what the probable commercial demand will

be for hog products within the provision year.
As there are so many elements entering into
the probable supply and prospective demand,
that we can not form a correct opinion in reference to the advance or decline in prices
other than by keeping in view the advance
and decline in the general course of prices
for hogs from year to year.

The price of the hog products have heretofore followed closely to the price of hogs.
Taking the last cycle in high prices for hogs,
we find that after the high priced year 1869,
the price of provisions declined in 1870, '71,
and '72, reaching the lowest limit in the summer of 1872. In the year 1873, when the
price of hogs advanced, provisions also advanced. Speculators are generally alive to
these facts, and on these periodical advances
they are ready and willing to operate, and invest as described in the following.

Chicago was well convinced in 1873, while
hogs were advancing in price, that " then was
the time in the price which, if taken at the
advance, leads on to fortune," and her operators went in on a bull speculation, and not
only bought up all the stock offered at current
rates, and contracted for all prospective supplies for Chicago, but went to New York and

bought up all stock offered, and all options, also went into European markets, and bought back their own stuff that had been shipped early and at low prices, and when the combination had secured the control of the markets, up went the price to extraordinary figures for the first year of advances in hogs and provisions after the former declines. Chicago was happy, and her speculators pocketed millions of money.

This Western bull campaign in provisions, with its lofty Texian horns tossing the markets to such dizzy heights as it did in 1873, could not have been successful, with all its financial strength, in any of the years of decline in the price of hogs.

The speculators who may attempt in 1876 or 1877 to bull the provision markets, can no more thrive and prosper than can swamp fever live on the lofty peaks of Chimborazo. And if this speculation be undertaken in these years, these Western operators will realize that they are mistaken, and will be slaughtered in this business as surely as were the deluded Hindo pilgrims mistaken in the means of salvation, and uselessly slaughtered when casting themselves between the wheels of the car of Juggernaut.

PANIC.

Panics in the commercial and financial world have been compared to comets in the astronomical world. It has been said of comets that they have no regularity of movement, no cycles, and that their movements are beyond the domain of astronomical science to find out.

It has been admitted by astronomers that the comet of 1874, named Coggia, was a new comet and a stranger; one that has not visited this part of the universe before within the history of mankind. However that may be, the writer claims that *Commercial Revulsions* in this country, which are attended with financial panics, can be predicted with much certainty; and the prediction in this book, of a commercial revulsion and financial crisis in 1891 is based upon the inevitable cycle which is ever true to the laws of trade, as affected and ruled by the operations of the laws of natural causes.

The panic of 1873 was a commercial revulsion; our paper money was not based upon specie, and the banks only suspended currency payments for a time in this crisis.

As it is not in the nature of things in each

succeeding cycle to operate in the same time and manner, the writer claims that the "signs of the times" indicate that the coming predicted disturbance in the business world will be not only an agricultural, manufacturing, mining, trading, and industrial revulsion, but also a *financial catastrophe*, producing a universal suspension of specie payments, and the closing up of all the banks in this country.

It is not necessary to give a detailed account of the effects of disorderly banking in our colonial and revolutionary history, and the different panics prior to the war of 1812, to establish cycles in commerce and finance.

Such a history would fill many pages without answering the purpose of this book, and would be as intricate and difficult to understand as the prices of stocks and gold in Wall Street, as the eternal fitness of things at that time were on trial, and necessarily unsettled, so far as man could understand.

The war of 1812 was the period in the history of the United States of America when it was deemed a necessity for this country to become a manufacturing nation, as a balance wheel to maintain the prosperity of agriculture and commerce, and also to declare her in-

7

dependence forever from any nation upon the earth.

It is a doleful commentary upon the times that such calamities in the history of our country, as hereafter mentioned, should have occurred amidst a profusion of all the elements of wealth, prosperity in trades and manufactures, and independence in the arts and sciences.

It will only be necessary for the purposes of this book to state that the business of this country before, during, and after the war of 1812 had culminated in the year 1819, as commercial history will show; and that a reaction in business followed this year, the beginning year in our cycles of commerce and panic.

However, we deem it important to notice at this period the operations of banking in brief as a good criterion of the prosperity and adversity in general business, and the fluctuations in the activity of industry and commerce.

In the Report of Finances for 1854, '55, it is stated that from the adoption of the Federal Constitution in 1787 to the year 1798, no people enjoyed more happiness or prosperity than the people of the United States, nor did any

country ever flourish more within that space
of time. During all this time, and up to the
year 1800, coin constituted the bulk of the
circulation; after this year the banks came,
and all things became changed; like the upas
tree, they have withered and impaired the
healthful condition of the country, destroyed
the credit and confidence which men had in
one another, and inflicted on the people political and pecuniary diseases of the most deadly
character.

The bank-note circulation began to exceed
the total specie in the country in the years
1815, '16, and '17, and in the year 1818, the
bank mania had reached its height; more
than two hundred new banks were projected
in various parts of the Union. The united
issues of the *United States Bank*, and of the
local banks, drove specie from the country in
large quantities, and in the year 1819, when
the culmination in general business had been
reached, and contraction of the currency began to be felt, multitudes of banks and indi-
viduals were broken. The panic producing a
disastrous revulsion in trade, caused the failure of nine-tenths of all the merchants in
this country and others engaged in business,
and spread ruin far and wide over the land

Two-thirds of the real estate passed from the hands of the owners to their creditors. Volumes would be required to portray the horrors and sufferings produced by this general commercial and financial revulsion in business and trade.

A bankɛr, in a letter to the Secretary of State, in 1830, describes the times as follows: " The disasters of 1819 which seriously affected the circumstances, property, and industry of every district of the United States will be long recollected.

" A sudden and pressing scarcity of money prevailed in the spring of 1822; numerous and very extensive failures took place in 1825; there was great revulsion among the banks and other monied institutions in 1826. The scarcity of money among the trades in 1827 was disastrous and alarming; 1828 was characterized by failures among the manufactures and trades in all branches of business. Lamentable and rapid succession of evil, and untoward events prejudicial to the progress of productive industry, and causing a baneful extension of embarrassment, insolvency, litigation, and dishonesty, alike subversive of social happiness and morals.

"Every intelligent mind must express regret

and astonishment at the occurrence of these
disasters in tranquil times and bountiful seasons, amongst enlightened, enterprising, and
industrious people, comparatively free from
taxation, unrestrained in pursuits, possessing
abundance of fertile lands and valuable min-
erals, with capital and capacity to improve,
and an ardent disposition to avail themselves
of the advantages of these great bounties."

After the year 1828 business continued to
be depressed, vibrating according to circumstances until 1834, a year of extreme dullness
in all branches of trade ; after which our stock
of precious metals increased very fast, business revived, and in the year 1835 and '36,
the imports of gold and silver increased to an
enormous extent ; as the banks increased their
reserves of specie, they also correspondingly
issued bank notes—each increased issue of
paper money led to the establishment of new
banks.

The State banks that had numbered in
1830 only three hundred and twenty-nine, with
a capital of one hundred and ten millions,
increased, according to the treasury report, by
the first of January, 1837, to six hundred and
twenty-four, or, including branches, to seven

hundred and eighty-eight, with a capital paid
in of two hundred and ninety millions.

Mark the result! and culmination!! a
panic!!! in the month of May, 1837, and
suspension of specie payments by all the
banks, and a general commercial revulsion
throughout the country, involving the fortunes
of merchants, manufacturers, and all classes
engaged in trade, in consequence of a ruinous
fall in prices. This year of reaction makes
the second year in our panic cycles, and is
eighteen years from 1819.

It is not necessary to go over almost the
same history again to show that business
was depressed, and trade was stagnant after
1837 down to the year 1843, and then up and
down to the year 1850, a year of extreme
dullness in all branches of trade and industry,
after which year a change came, and business
was again prosperous to the year 1857, when
we again experienced a commercial and financial crisis and reaction, not only in this country
but all over the world, making the third year
in our cycles, and twenty years from 1837.

History repeats itself with marvelous accuracy in detail from one panic year to another.
The general direction of business after the
panic of 1857 was on the same downward

grade that had characterized the times after
the panics of 1819 and 1837, until all business
had culminated in depression in the year
1861, after which trade again improved, and
was very active during the war of rebellion and
up to the year 1865, when a temporary reaction set in ; and, reader, let me observe here,
that if then had been the time for a commercial revulsion and panic in money, the catastrophe would have been the most deplorable
national calamity upon record. However, the
cycle was not then complete, and the commerce and trade of the country continued to
be semi-prosperous until 1870, after which
year commercial activity was the order of the
day, all branches of business and manufacture
flourished and was prosperous; our railroad
building was astonishing in the world in the
years 1871, '72; but the end must come, and in
September, 1873, we had the culmination—a
crushing panic, and reaction in all trades,
manufactures, railroads, and industries, which
is still going on, and we have not yet reached
hard pan.

These are facts of late history, and are so
fresh in the recollection of the mind of the
reader, that it is only necessary to refer to
them. The panic of 1873 makes the fourth

year in our panic cycles, **and sixteen years**
from 1857.

As to whether it is the paper money or the
manufacturing and trading industries of the
country, which call out and into use the paper money that produce these periodical in-
flations and contractions, by which trade is
stimulated and deranged, and extremes in
business activity is brought about, is a matter for the statesman and historian to ascertain and record; it is only sufficient for our
present purpose to point out the panic years,
and to show that the preceding years were
prosperous and profitable years in trade;
while the succeeding years, for a certain
length of time, were years of depression and
loss in business; and we observe that since
the business of the country has abandoned
specie as a currency, and adopted paper
money in lieu thereof, the manufacturing
interests have attained larger proportions,
and that there are more regularity and system
in the return of the advance and decline in
general business, and that the culminating
years in activity and depression can be calculated and ascertained with greater certainty.

The CYCLES in PANICS with the cycles of
PIG-IRON in the *same scale.*

20 — 1893

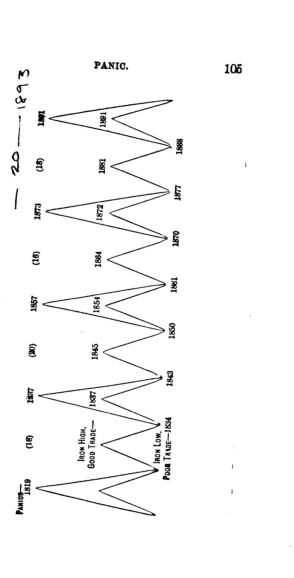

The panics of 1819, '37, '57, and '73, during this period of years, stand out upon the pages of the history of this country in their magnitude compared with other panics, as the planet Jupiter compares with the lesser planets in our solar system.

Commencing with the commercial revulsion of 1819, we find it was eighteen years to the crisis of 1837; twenty years to the crisis of 1857; and sixteen years to the crisis of 1873— making the order of cycles sixteen, eighteen, and twenty years and repeat. The cycle of twenty years was completed in 1857, and the cycle of sixteen years ending in 1873, was the commencement of the repetition of the same order. It takes panics fifty-four years in their order to make a revolution, or to return in the same order; the present cycle consisting of eighteen years will end in 1891, when the next panic will burst upon us with all its train of woes.

Returning to the bottom of the scale, there we find the years of POOR TRADE and HARD TIMES; between panic years in the scale there are two low points, indicating two different times of depression in the iron business; these low points indicate the hard pan years in general business. Confidence after these years,

especially after the latter, exercises its empire
and casts overboard the incubus that has
weighed down enterprise and energy; these
years are the ending of the declines, the beginning of better prices and more prosperous
times. The year 1877 is the next low point
in our scale for price of pig-iron. This year
will be a dull and unprofitable year for the
iron trade, and also for general business.

The next high point will be 1881, a prosperous year for the iron business. However, in
the year 1882, and the six succeeding years
running to 1888, like the years after 1854 and
1864, we may look for squalls in the money
market, blue-Mondays, black-Fridays, and tornadoes in banking, and the first financial flury
under the coming specie basis, which will
have to rest upon a confidence artificially
created and artificially supported, unless the
currency is contracted to that minimum which
would prostrate the industries of the country,
paralyze the life and energy of our people, and
produce convulsions and depressions only
equaled in the years succeeding 1819, '37, and
'57, filling up the pages of history with commercial and financial disasters, as they were
filled up to 1834 and 1850. After the year
1888 the price of pig-iron will advance, all

business will be prosperous, corn and hogs
will be on the advance, agriculture and manufacture will be active, all trades and industries
will make money up to the year 1891, when
we predict a panic which will not be confined
to the United States, or this continent, but
will sweep over the world like the panics of
1819 and 1857, and will be felt with equal
severity in other countries.

Since 1819, panics burst upon us after the
price of pig-iron had commenced to decline,
and therefore it is not chargeable to a general
panic as the direct cause of the price of iron
taking the descending scale; the price declines
without a general panic, (see scale after 1845,
and '64,) and the same will be the case in 1881.
In 1891, the commencement of the decline in
the price of pig-iron will precede the panic of
September or October of that year.

The writer claims that the iron trade is the
chief and ruling industry in this country, if
not in the world. Iron is the most useful of
all metals, in fact the bone and sinew of our
civilization, and the most important element
of progress, as seen in the sewing machine,
reaper and mower, spinning-jenny, power
loom, steamboat, railroad, land and submarine
telegraph. And as the iron industry raises or

falls in the scale of prosperity, so does the
general business of the country. Pig-iron is
our north star to guide us over the dangerous
roads of commerce. It is the barometer of
trade, and as the sudden falling of the mercury denotes violent changes in the atmos-
pherical world, so does the periodical decline
in the price of pig-iron indicate panic, depression, and general stagnation in business.

The United States of America will in the
future surpass all the world besides, in the
production of pig-iron and in the manufacture
of its products; and if this trade could be established upon a firm basis, and the labor
employed in dull times until it has accumulated capital, with the ingenuity, invention,
and skill of the indomitable Yankee in the
complex processes of its manufacture, with
our abundance of cheap raw material, and by
the aid of natural gas for fuel as lately and
successfully applied at Pittsburg, a thorough
knowledge of the ups and downs of prices in
the markets and cycles of good and bad trade,
this industry in this country in its colossal
proportions, would in a short time, defy the
world's competition, give us better and
cheaper iron; give more steadiness to prices,

and greatly mitigate the consequences of periodical crises and depressions.

The highest and lowest prices in the cycles of high and low priced years for iron are in a progressive order, as reported in the monthly price tables of the Iron and Steel Association. The high prices commencing in January, 1837, going over to May in 1845, to June in 1854, to August in 1864, and to September in 1872. The low prices, commencing in April, 1834, reaching to July in 1843, to July in 1850, to October in 1861, and December in 1870; showing that each cycle extends a fraction over the required years. The low prices for 1877 will run into January of 1878.

The panic of 1819 began early in the year, and that of 1837 in May, and of 1857 in September, and of 1873 in September. The price of pig-iron in 1881 will not reach the maximum until September; after that month it will begin to decline. The price of pig-iron in 1891 will not begin to decline before September, as the panic will not appear before that month in that year.

Astronomy tells us that eclipses return in the same order every eighteen years. Every eclipse within this period of eighteen years belongs to a separate series of eclipses; that is,

there is but one eclipse during the eighteen
years which belong to the same series. This
periodical return was discovered by the an-
cients, and by this rule they were able to foretell the appearance of many of the eclipses
years in advance; and by close observation
through many centuries, astronomers at this
day can foretell the exact hour and minute of
the appearance of any or all the eclipses.
Other cycles of motion in the heavens vary in
their particular order of series. Science will
yet show that there is a reality in the connec-
tion between human events and the operations
of nature; the causes and the laws by which
they operate we are now ignorant of.

The cycles in panics and ups and downs in
prices of agricultural and manufactured articles are but the effects of a cause, which is
manifested in periods of sixteen, eighteen and
twenty years in panics; that return in the same
order every fifty-four years, in periods of eight,
nine, and ten years in the price of pig-iron;
which return in the same order every twenty-
seven years, and down to five and six years in
the price of corn and hogs; which return in
the same order every eleven years; and by a
series of observation in the future, the particular month and day could be ascertained when

these changes in the ups and downs in prices
will occur. When once these cycles are defined, ascertained, and calculated upon to a
month and day, by a careful compilation of
prices in each cycle, and the natural causes
producing them discovered and verified, then
their return can be calculated to continue in
that exact order as long as other cycles in motion; as they are the effects of other motions,
and will return with as much certainty and
astronomical exactness, as the return of the
eclipses of the sun and moon; and it does not require a belief in the fabulous to have faith in
their periodical appearance. These cycles in the
operations of cause and effect have always existed. There has been no confusion. Man has
been continually making discoveries of the
manner in which the laws of nature operate.

In my predictions I stated that 1876 and '77,
would be years of great depression in general
business, and that there would be many failures in these years; they will come at the end
of the five years' decline in the price of pig-
iron; and it does not require a gift of prophecy
to foretell many failures in all of these years.

The "signs of the times" can be calculated
by comparing 1876 and 1877 with other years
after commercial panics, and the fall in the

price of pig-iron—for instance, 1842, '43, and
1860, '61—and the state of business preceding
these years, remembering that 1876 is presidential year, and that presidential years like
1820, 1840, and 1860, immediately succeeding
commercial revulsions, are years of depression
in business, the uncertainty of the times and
of future legislation clogs the wheels of
commerce and stops business. "Hard times"
and "dull trade" are surely upon us for the
next two years. The working man who depends upon his labor for his living, especially they who are engaged in the iron trade,
surely have a dreary prospect—compelled by
low wages to practice the most rigid economy
in the necessaries of life, in the use of bad
flour, black molasses, pressed shoulders, and
store pay. And in the depression of the agricultural, manufacturing, and industrial interests, as they will be depressed all over the
land in the next two years, the sting of hard
times will come to every man's home.

In all these years of reaction and depression
in general business, Providence works upon
the minds of men, as witnessed at the present
time by the religious excitement in the East,
created by the evangelists Moody and Sankey,
as instruments in the hands of God to start in

motion a religious wave that will in the next two years sweep over the entire western country.—Men in time of trouble put more trust in God, and are inclined to more thoughtfulness.

The writer stated in his predictions that notwithstanding the resumption of specie payments, the price of iron and hogs will be higher in 1879 than in 1878. The price of iron and hogs will have already suffered a diminution in premium and price in their low priced year 1877. It is natural for prices to advance in 1878, 1879, and 1880, and no legislative act can prevent it. The return to specie payments will give confidence in business and stability to trade.

Congress made a mistake in not fixing January 1, 1878, as the time for the resumption of specie payments; this delay will cause the government and people to lose twelve months of recuperative strength in the great commercial and financial battle of 1891.

January 1, 1878, is the time when all needful and necessary contraction of the currency for a specie basis will be in conformity with the universal contraction of business, which will have been going on ever since the revulsion of 1873, and when general depression will have reached the very bottom of hard pan, and when the times will demand that contraction in trade and currency must cease, and the ending of the cycle in low prices for pig-iron, the great jupiter of trade.

The combined interests of the people will demand that this incubus and scare-crow upon industry and trade be confined to the shortest period consistent with the times, and that there be no contraction after the year 1877. Agriculture, manufacture, mining, commerce, finance, and the cycles of high heaven demand it; to restore business confidence; to relieve general distress, and to repair national and individual disaster.

Commercial panic is the reaction from over trading and over expansion of credit and confidence, an excess of commerce and finance. Political economy abounds in theories to explain the cause of panics. It is not necessary to look about for a cause; commercial and financial revulsions are the consequences of many causes.

When the price of iron begins to decline there is a panic in iron. When the price of hogs commence to decline there is a panic in hogs. When the price of cotton, wool, wheat, or any product begins to fall, there is a panic in that particular article; the supply exceeds the demand. Prosperity in the aggregate creates general confidence, and expands credit, and this swells the prosperity, increases the demand for money, inducing banks to extend their issues and loans to the utmost, until the climax is reached; then comes the panic, the inevitable crisis and reaction; the pressure to realize produces a decline in prices; confidence is lost, capital, ever sensitive, withdraws; a run commences on the banks, ending in financial and commercial disaster.

Commercial revulsions are governed by a law beyond the control of man, and are confined to no creed, party, or politics.

The panic of 1819 was in Monroe's administration; that of 1837 in Martin Van Buren's; of 1857 in James Buchanan's; and of 1873 in U. S. Grant's.

No governmental or congressional subsidies; no legislative enactments, tariffs, or currencies; no financial syndicates, convertible or interchangeable bonds; no bribery of legislators or betrayal of constituents can arrest or change their course.

When the period arrives for a panic, any breeze or signal, no matter what reverses the engine, the times take the downward grade,

and there is no general recovery until we
hear pig-iron demanding

"WATCHMAN! WHAT OF THE NIGHT?"

This ideal will have been standing out
upon the dome of the weather-beaten tower of
time, gazing into the dim vista of the future,
for five long years of disaster and ruin, waiting for the period foreseen and predicted,
when the glimmer of the year 1878 can be
discerned in the eastern horizon, not a mete-
oric flash which illumes the night with a
transient and uncertain glow; but the continued morning radiance, which is the fore-
runner of the full light and glory of a bright
noon-day—will then exclaim AROUSE, PIG-
IRON! monarch of business! come forth from
the chambers of thy slumbering silence, the
dawn of a new era is at hand! hogs, corn, and
cotton fall into line, and start in motion the
wheels of commerce, industry, and trade!

The resumption of trade and industry in
the year 1878 must go on; the Gibraltar of
hard times will be passed in 1877; the mills
and furnaces will start up; the price of pig-
iron, hogs, corn, and provisions will be on
the advance. Agriculture, manufacture, mining, commerce, and finance, will begin to

prosper; the industries of all this country will
be born of new life, and with our finances
upon a sound basis, and a stop put to the
enormous importation of foreign goods, that
we can manufacture ourselves, which will
give us the balance of trade, and enable us to
keep our gold at home, and a general knowledge among the people of the duration of the
ups and downs in prices, and when we may
expect the return of commercial panics—this
country with its forty millions of population,
seventy thousand miles of railway, and two
hundred millions of acres of cultivated land,
will prosper and advance beyond any nation
which has appeared in all ages of the world,
and the chronicles of its future history, if
well written, will rival the stories of oriental
imagination.

THEORY.

We have had to hunt down PRICE CYCLES
by establishing periodicity in high and low
priced years; the length of the different
periods in which they have repeated themselves, and by indisputable dates, facts, and
figures, demonstrating their regularity.

The cause producing the periodicity and
length of these cycles may be found in our

solar system. The writer does not claim a
knowledge of the causes and conditions under
which they occur, and the reasons why they
occur; *meteorological scientists* have been laboring and exploring the records of all ages to
discover a *Meteorological Cycle*—the great desideratum of the age.

In the ELEMENTS OF METEOROLOGY, by Prof.
John H. Tice, of St. Louis, Mo., published in
1875, are meteorological cycles, demonstrated
and verified according to his theory, which is
that *Planetary Equinoxes* are the causes of the
disturbance to which our earth and atmosphere is periodically subject.

That all the elements of disturbance are
physically interwoven with and inseparable
from the planetary system, and that Jupiter
at his equinoctial points suffers physical perturbations both in his body and atmosphere,
probably more intense than the disturbances
at our equinoxes. These cause similar atmos-
pherical and physical paroxysms in Jupiter,
as our equinoctial disturbances do; namely,
electric and magnetic storms and earthquakes
in the body of the planet; and in the atmosphere, violent tornadoes and hurricanes, ac-
companied with terrible electric explosions,
heavy rain-falls and hail storms, and that

these equinoctial disturbances in Jupiter affect the sun, and through the sun the solar system. The result upon the earth and its atmosphere is an enormous increase of electric intensity. Gives the equinoxes of Vulcan, Mercury, Venus, Earth, Mars, Jupiter, and Saturn, and also a historical record of auroras, sun-spots, earthquakes, magnetic disturbances, cyclones, rain-falls, and hail storms, in verification of his cycle, and demonstrates that Jupiter is the cause of the atmospheric, tellurie, and solar perturbations that occur once and in a modified form twice in every one of his orbital revolutions, and that the maximum disturbance upon the earth must occur at or near Jupiter's equinox, and that the energy of the equinox of any planet is intensified when that of another occurs at or about the same time. Fixes 11,86 years as the length of the Jupiter year, and names it the Jovial Cycle, and assumes that on the following years in this century have occurred, and will occur, the Jovial Major Equinox :

1800.58	1859.88
1812.44	1871.74
1824.30	1883.60
1836.16	1895.46
1848.02	

The cycles of 11 years in the price of corn and hogs, 27 years in the price of pig-iron, and 54 years in general business, can not be accounted for upon any known theory in the operations of trade. Therefore we must look elsewhere for a cause and solution of the problem.

The fact of the existence of these cycles is patent to any close observer, and as to whether any hypothesis or theory would be of practical utility when not a demonstrated and *verified* truth, is for the reader to determine.

In our 11 year cycles commencing in 1836, and running to 1847, '58, and '69, we observe that our cycles fall behind the Jovial Cycle. We have not the daily or monthly prices for corn and hogs, so as to ascertain if there are fractions of a year in our cycles; if there should be, they would be found to be small. We know there are fractions in the cycles for pig-iron extending over four months from 1837 to 1845, and in other cycles from one to two months, but not sufficient fractions in any cycle within the past forty years, and will not be before 1891, to change the number of years in any high priced year cycle of either hogs or pig-iron.

The meteorological cycle, as verified **by** Prof. Tice, seems to be well demonstrated by his array of historical facts.

His forecasts of the weather during the year 1875 was verified with surprising accuracy, and we have no doubt that his theory in regard to sun-spots, earthquakes, auroras, and magnetic disturbances is well confirmed. However, it is to be considered that other elements and influences may operate to cause abundance or scarcity in stock and grain crops.

Facts are the data of all just reasoning, and the primary elements of all real knowledge. The fact seems to be philosophically certain that all the planets which compose our solar system are essential to that system : the sun to the planets, the planets to the sun, and all to each other; and when certain combinations are ascertained which produce one legitimate invariable manifestation from an analysis of the operations of the combined solar system, then we may be enabled to discover the cause producing our price cycles, and the length of their duration.

It is evident from our showing of the ups and downs in prices, and the high and low priced years, that these cycles repeat them-

selves in definite length; and without determining a fixed and exciting cause for their
existence, or attempting to verify theories of
which we are distrustful, we will risk our
reputation as a prophet, and our chances for
success in business upon our 11 year cycle in
corn and hogs; in our 27 year cycle in pig-
iron, and in our 54 year cycle in general
trade, upon which we have operated with success in the past.

Modern facilities have brought the ends of
the earth together, and nearly obliterated the
cycles in famine and bread riots, but in turn
have developed well defined cycles in prices.
By the aid of steam and electricity, a de-
ficiency in one part of the earth is soon supplied by the surplus of another; therefore,
natural productions are more equalized over
the country; and as the average aggregate
yearly amount is regulated by productive and
unproductive seasons, prices follow nature
more closely than formerly, and their cycles
must correspond very closely with meteorological cycles.

The influence of the sun-spot period upon
production and prices, has formed the subject
of numerous discussions during the present
century; and it is a singular fact that scien-

tists have made the discovery that large and
small crops have occurred at intervals approx-
imating to eleven years, the average length of
the sun-spot period. It may be a meteorological fact that Jupiter is the ruling element in
our price cycles of natural productions; while
also it may be suggested that Saturn exerts an
influence regulating the cycles in manufacture and trade.

Herschel and Leverrier, away out in the
regions of immensity, beyond the range of
human eyesight, may send forth an electric
influence affecting Jupiter, Saturn, and, in
turn, the Earth. Heathen mythology claimed
that Saturn was the deity who presided over
time, as he was the most distant planet from
the earth of any that are visible to the naked
eye, and requiring twenty-nine years to make
a revolution around the sun. Saturn appears
to have been king of Crete, in whose time iron
was said to have been discovered on Mount
Ida, owing to a fire by lightning producing a
conflagration in the woods. Vulcan wrought
the new iron mines and made iron imple-
ments. Ancient astrology claimed to foretell
future events by the motion of the stars, and
in this they were not far wrong, although they
were not regulated in their predictions by

cycles in motion, but by certain changes in the stars at certain times, aided by the celestial globe, and approaches, recessions, and aspects of the planets. Ancient astrology is now being superceded by modern science. All great events and convulsions in nature are now being explained and accounted for upon fixed physical causes.

The deluge of Moses, if we look for a physical cause, can be found in the precession of the equinoxes. The perihelion having a period of over 25,000 years, crossed the equator when the translation of the ocean from the northern to the southern hemisphere, would necessarily produce wrecks of countries, great physical changés, and floods upon the earth. For all history concurs in describing a deluge, and science demands its recurrence about every 12,000 years.

CONCLUSION.

In view of the immensity of the interests involved, and the magnitude of the gains or losses incurred in the advance and decline of each price and panic cycle, and the consequences of the effects upon all business and trade, well might we be surprised and aston-

ished at the opportunities afforded for accumulation and the chances for disaster, that by
rule of cycles we are compelled to predict.

Persons who undertake to search for coal
outside of the coal fields, to mine for ore outside of the iron region, or prospect for any
mineral by which through ignorance of the
teachings of geology, they would be constantly
led to squander their means for that which
they can not find—could be compared to a
person who undertakes to make money during
the decline of prices. Failures in business are
caused principally by our ignorance of *when*
the ups and downs in prices are to take place.
It has been stated that in the city of Boston,
in a series of forty years after the year 1800,
that only five in one hundred men remained
in business; they had all in that time failed
or died destitute of property. It has been
stated and ascertained that not more than one
per cent of the best class of merchants escape
from failing in Philadelphia, and that not
more than two per cent of the merchants of
New York ultimately retire on an independence during periods of twenty-five and thirty
years. In Cincinnati, out of a list of some
four hundred of the principal business men
who were in trade in that city at a certain

period, there were only five in business at the end of twenty years from that date. Such is mercantile success, and we see the same repeated in all the leading and different branches of trade.

As compiled by Dunn, Barlow & Co., of New York City, for the year 1873, throughout the country there were 5,183 failures of business men, with liabilities aggregating to $228,499-000; for the year 1874 there were 5,830 failures, with liabilities of $155,239,900; and the indications of reports for 1875, are that the failures will number as many as in the former years. The greater proportion of these failures were brought about by losses sustained in the shrinkage of values, and decline of prices in each price and panic cycle. The people seem ignorant of the terrible teachings of history, and few are prepared to take advantage of these turns in trade; and the great majority, through ignorance of the time when the ups and down in prices are to take place, are caught with incomplete enterprises upon their hands.

It is noticed that the great majority of the business men of broken down fortunes, have become so not by accident, but by dealing too largely when prices were on the decline. In

the general declines of business after the
panics of 1819, '37, '57, and '73, the loss to the
nation through non-employment of labor and
in various ways, is estimated to aggregate a
sufficient sum in each of these reactions to
pay our national debt. George Peabody laid
the foundation of his fortune by buying American securities in one of our commercial
depressions, the price which, taken at the
advance, led him on to competence.

READER, if you are young, life is short. You
can not afford to make any mistakes, or miss
any opportunities. You must take the tide
at the advance. You can not wait a life time
for the results of your experience; you must
act upon what others know, or your life will
be spent to little use and without much accumulation of property. The cycles of prosperity and adversity alternate inside of every
ten years; but few of these prosperous decades
are yours in an active business life; therefore
do not waste your strength, or impair your
energies on these periodic declines, as fore-
shadowed in the future by the bright written
pages of past history.

Barnum has well said, in his celebrated
lecture on the art of money getting, "You can
not accumulate a fortune by taking the road

that leads to poverty." The whole history of
trade and commerce is full with the records of
disaster, which has been brought about by mistakes of men who could not read the letters
upon the sign posts; while on the other hand
our libraries are crowded with the chronology
of man's success in business and trade, by
taking the price and times at the advance,
which leads on to fortune.

Within the present century the increase of
knowledge, improvements in machinery, and
the discoveries in the arts and sciences, have
advanced with a speed unparalleled in the
annals of history. New light in various departments of human activity is now rapidly
and continually breaking in upon the world.
The invention of the steamboat, railroad, and
telegraph, have imparted astonishing lessons
to mankind. Each discovery of the laws of
nature unfolds to the mind of man, new and
exalting evidences of the wisdom of the Crea-
tor. Astronomers who attempt to explore the
immensity of the starry regions; to discover
unseen and unknown worlds, and to find out
the ways of God in the wonders of the heavens,
are not in this enlightened age denounced as
false philosophers and charged with an im-
pious invasion of the domain of God. Each

rising science has fought and struggled with
superstition and ignorance; and in all ages no
effort has been spared to blast them in the bud
of their being, or crush them in the cradle of
their infancy.

It has only been a short time before the
present century, that if any one had predicted
the crossing of the ocean in a vessel driven by
steam, or of conveying news by electric agency
around the earth, over the land and under the
water in advance of time, or of daguerreotyp-
ing the human face on a metallic plate by the
light of the sun, and then chemically fixing
it there; or of forecasting the future of the
weather; production and prices by the rule of
cycles as regulated by providence; such persons would have been considered visionary,
their predictions regarded as contemptibly
absurd; their authors the most disingenious
of men, and their theories and systems treated
with persecution and ridicule.

The day is past for men to be forced to drink
the juice of the hemlock for having peculiar
notions of Deity, and sent in chains to the
gallows, or imprisoned in gloomy dungeons
for announcing scientific discoveries. Galileo
was condemned by the inquisition of Rome for
teaching the doctrine of the earth's revolu-

tions.   Galileo was right, and the world moves.

Science has many things to achieve in agriculture, manufacture, mining, and commerce. The science of *price cycles* is yet in the cradle of its infancy, but waiting its time to mature full development, to unfold its principles, and declare its oracles to all mankind, and to demonstrate that the causes and the laws of nature in production are not past finding out; and that man in his onward path of progress, with the aid of electric science, will ultimately grasp the future, and make plain all the ways of God; which, when accomplished in this world, will be the acme of human knowledge, the consummation of human perfection, and the end of human destiny.

ADDENDA, 1884.

To comply with an urgent demand from many business men for a new edition of these Prophecies, with tables brought down to date, the author has consented to make some additions, and add a chapter on Railroad Stocks. The old edition is left as it was originally published in 1876.

While it has been an accepted saying, that history repeats itself, it has never been attempted heretofore to show how, and say when, it was systematically done, so as to extend it into the future—until the writer, in 1876, introduced to the public this little book, showing, by cycles made in the ups and downs in prices and in general business, how and when the times would repeat themselves in the future, which by the test of the past eight years, is pronounced, by intelligent and thinking business men, to be one of the most remarkable commercial discoveries of this country.

This book has been read by many able men, and they are puzzled at the results, as showing powerfully what they did not believe existed, and so at variance with received opinions, they seem willing, from choice, to disbelieve it, if it were possible, but seeing the predictions and repetitions justified by events, are disposed to give the author great glory.

The discovery of this so-called law of repetition, pertaining to business life, one would say can not be, for how the times change from war and other causes. The answer is: that the law has acted for fifty years, or as long as we have had any reliable statistics to test it; and this action has been going on through the introduction of railroads, steamships, the electric telegraph and cable, the panics of 1837, 1857 and 1873; also, through the Mexican war and our own civil war, and all else that has occurred to oppose such regularity. And what more can a reasonable person ask to prevent its action? And yet it rides triumphant over all, and asserts itself up to the present time in a wonderful manner.

In the commodity of Iron, the author takes the best tables this country affords, and with the formation of which he has nothing to do, viz.: those compiled by the American Iron and Steel Association of Philadelphia, and from these prices, for the past fifty years, are shown the highest and lowest years, which are systematically apart, forming cycles which repeat themselves at certain fixed periods. These are facts, and if facts, they are true, whether they are believed or not.

Iron is the strongest element of general business; and when the price of iron is advancing and high, general business is always prosperous, and labor finds steady and remunerative employment. On the contrary, when iron is de-declining and low, general business languishes and labor suffers its worst. This fact has been invariably the case during the whole history of the United States; and it is the great desideratum of the age to discover the operation of a repetition in this commodity, and place it intelligently before the public, so that business men can shape their affairs in accordance with it.

The uncertainty heretofore of all manufacturing business, for a want of the knowledge of how long good trade or poor trade would continue, of which it seems our sharpest and most experienced men have made serious and fatal mistakes, will now, by this knowledge of repetition, be enabled to forecast the run of future business, and give them more confidence by knowing when to contract or expand their operations.

Many a chance for a fortune is lost through over caution; and many a fortune is lost through being over sanguine, without a sure guide gained by the known laws of the operations of the past. The height and culmination of a speculative era is the best time for sinking capital beyond the hope of recovery, and commercial depression affords the best opportunity for profitable investment, as these pages show under the head of Iron and Panic.

PROPHECIES VERIFIED.

The author predicted, in 1875, that there would be a continuation of the depression in iron and general business to extend through 1876 and 1877—which prophecies were fulfilled.

The further prediction then, was that prices would commence to advance in 1878—which they did. The advance in iron commenced in the latter part of 1878, while railroad stocks had reached their lowest limit of decline in 1877. These years—1877 and 1878—were the end of the great commercial depression foreseen and predicted by the writer.

The remarkable part of this prediction was in forecasting a turn in business affairs, and higher prices to follow, in spite of resumption of spe-

cie payments. The general opinion at that
time, was that resumption meant contraction
and lower prices.

During 1879 and 1880, the times improved
and prices advanced, just as predicted. All
trades and industries were active through these
years. Iron reached its highest price in 1880,
and stocks in 1881.

The prediction also was that after 1881 prices
would decline and the times grow worse, which
prediction has been verified down to this date.

The two important points, one of depression
in 1877, and the commencement of better times
in 1878, and to follow, and the other of great
business activity and culmination in 1881, and
the commencement of dull and poor trade, and
to follow after that year, have been substantially
verified.

On page 49, of this book, there is said, " that
the years 1882, '83, '84, '85, '86, '87 and '88, will
be years of decline in the price of pig-iron, and
years of depression in this business." Now, let
us see what the secretary of the Iron and Steel
Association says in his report made in 1883 :
" In our last annual report, in June, 1882, the
fact was noted, that the extraordinary activity
in our iron and steel industries, which had commenced in 1879, had culminated early in 1882,

when the wants of consumers became less urgent and prices generally began to decline.
This reaction was not sudden nor violent, but
was, indeed, so gradual and tranquil that it not
only, for some time, excited no apprehension of
impending stringency, but was actually imper-
ceptible to many manufacturers whose books
still continued to receive liberal orders at satis-
factory prices. After the resumption of activity
in the rolling mills, the price of rolled iron and
pig-iron declined until the close of the year,
and in November and December the market for
these products was greatly depressed. Steel
rails, which were the first of all iron and steel
products to weaken in price—quotations having
slightly receded as early as December, 1881—
steadily declined in price throughout the whole
year, the sharpest decline occurring in November and December, when the demand for future
delivery almost came to an end. At the beginning of December, 1881, the average price of
steel rails, at the mills, was $60 a ton; but in
December, 1882, the average price was only $39.
In all the fluctuations of prices of iron and steel
that have taken place in this country, we know
of none so sweeping as this decline in the price
of steel rails, if we except the fluctuations of
1879 and 1880, and many of these were entirely

speculative. The causes which contributed to
the serious, but in no sense disastrous, reaction
in our iron and steel industries, in 1882, were
many and various."

The lowest limit for pig-iron being touched a
few months later, and the highest daily price
earlier than the specified limitations and culmi-
nations in predictions made for the years 1877
and 1881, do not affect the verification of the
repetitions, as there were very important causes
why these limits were prolonged and hastened
a few months. In whatever can not be as exact as two and two are four, is no reason why
'tis false and should be abandoned.

Let the thinking mind of any far-seeing business man call into action all his mental energies
—gird himself to the herculean task; let him
put forth his proudest thought, grasp the subject with a giant arm, and endeavor to forecast
the future ups and downs of iron and general
business in this country for the next ten years,
without the help of cycles and this law of repetition, as the author has set forth in these
pages, and see how wide he will miss the mark.

A prominent grain merchant, when questions in regard to the probable effect of a European war upon the market for American bread-
stuffs, replied that definite predictions could be

obtained only from merchants who had been but a short time in the business ; the older he grew the more ignorant he became concerning the future.

SIGNS OF THE TIMES.

The price of iron has steadily fallen through the year 1883.

That the times are dull, can not be disputed. We have now the anamoly of an easy money market and hard times.   From month to month, since 1881, commodities have fallen in price, wages have been cut down, manufactories closed, workmen thrown out of employment, and at the present time the cities fairly swarm with a grand army of the unemployed.   There has not been for years a greater scarcity of trade bills, so little demand for the deposits that banks and discount houses hold.   Unsound firms and mismanaged corporations are failing daily, a series of commercial failures larger than ever in this country.   A merchant contemplating an opening up of a new department in trade, postpones it ; a manufacturer needing new machinery, puts off the purchase of it ; a man intending to build a new house, waits.   All these indicate poor trade and great prostration

in business. And this state of affairs in this
country, which we are compelled to describe as
it actually exists, is likely to continue until we
have a turn in iron for great activity, which can
not come until 1888, as pointed out by the repetitions of the past.

All persons who are interested in pig-iron
and railroad and other securities, are anxiously
inquiring into the probabilities of iron declining
more. With over one-third of the blast furnaces
in this country standing idle, and the greater
number of those in blast struggling to pay expenses, this inquiry is one of great and ex-
ceeding interest.

The writer now proceeds to outline the future
condition of trade, from this time to the close of
this century.

1884.

Presidential year. The absorbing topic.
What party is going to administer the Government for the next four years to be decided in
the election this fall, will be a disturbing element in business, and will have the effect of
casting its withering shadow before it, clogging
the wheels of commerce and manufacture;
hence, dull trade. Iron will continue to droop,
with lower prices.

1885.

This year will show some resumption in the business of the country, the election being over and out of the way. There will be a little higher average for iron for this year, and this year only, with railroad stocks higher than in 1884.

1886.

A renewal of depression in the iron and general business, and a lower average for iron. Free-trade agitation and legislation by Congress. The low duty tariffs have been shameful failures in this country, reducing the Government and people to a deplorable condition. The low-tariff era, from 1857 to 1861, was one of the darkest periods ever seen by the laboring people of America. Stocks lower.

1887.

Continuation of the same dull trade of 1886, with no hope for iron this year.

1888.

Presidential year; all business prostrated and exhausted. A general complaint of hard times all over the country. Banks failing and stocks to their lowest point. Iron and stocks will touch their lowest limit in this decline, and turn *upward in this year.*

1889.

A great speculative era opening up. Hurrah, for business! Iron **advances.** Now for a BOOM.

1890.

Great activity in general business. Iron and stocks advancing and bounding upward, from the beginning to the ending of this year. A repetition of the year 1879.

1891.

This era of speculation and great prosperity comes to a close this year with a PANIC. A commercial revulsion and general reaction in all business after this year, and down goes trade for a series of years.

1892, 1893, 1894, 1895, 1896, 1897.

Dull years and poor trade.

1898, 1899.

Good trade and an active business in all industries, winding up this 19th century in the height of a speculative era.

It will be noticed that there are to be only two period of years, from this time until 1900 when we will have great activity in general business, and these are given below in the future.

The former prominent active business periods of advances in iron were from

1834 to 1837. — •‹
1843 to 1845. -- ‹.
1850 to 1854.   ‹
1861 to 1864. - ‹:
1870 to 1872.   ‹ ‹
1878 to 1880.   ‹.

FUTURE.
1888 to 1891.
1897 to 1899.

It seems from the above that the advance and activity in iron is but a few months at a time, while the periods of decline are numbered by years and of long duration. However, it should not be a subject of too much complaint, when we think of the locust—only a week's song in every seventeen years.

AVERAGE YEARLY PRICES FOR PIG-IRON.

YEARS.	*PRICE.*	*TONS.*	*YEARS.*	*PRICE.*	*TONS.*
1844	25¾	. . .	1863	35¼	947,604
1845	29¼	. . .	1864	59¼	1,135,996
1846	27⅞	. . .	1865	46⅛	931 582
1847	30¼ .	. . .	1866	46⅞	1,350,343
1848	26½	. . .	1867	44⅛	1,461,626
1849	22¾	; . .	1868	39¼	1,603,000
1850	20⅞	. . .	1869	40⅝	1,916,641
1851	21⅜	. . .	1870	33¼	1,865,000
1852	22⅝	. . .	1871	35⅛	1,911,608
1853	36⅛	. . .	1872	48⅞	2,854,558
1854	36⅞	736,218	1873	42¾	2,868 278
1855	27¾	784,178	1874	30¼	2,689,413
1856	27⅛	883,137	1875	25½	2,266,581
1857	26⅜	798,157	1876	22¼	2,093,236
1858	22¼	705,094	1877	18⅞	2 314,585
1859	23⅜	840,627	1878	17⅝	2,577,361
1860	22¾	919,770	1879	21½	3,070,875
1861	20¼	731,544	1880	28½	4,295,414
1862	23⅞	787,662	1881	25⅛	4,641,564
			1882	25¾	5,178,122

FAILURES.

As compiled by R. G. Dun & Co., of New York City, for the year 1883, there were over nine thousand traders failed in business; and, with the exception of the year 1878, there were more failures in number in 1883 than in any year in the history of this country.

To quote from their circular of January, 1884 : " Under such circumstancess the inquiry is a most anxious one, as to what is the actual business outlook for the opening year. If, with all that has happencd in the past of a favorable character, disasters of such magnitude have occured, what is to be expected with the loss of confidence which these calamities have caused, with the restricted credit accomodation, lessened business, and the steady depreciation in values, which seem to be the daily experience."

Now, the writer undertakes to state, that the capacity of this country to over produce is out of all proportion to the power and ability to consume.

This fact was very plainly exemplified in the iron business during 1879. Just so soon as the people saw that iron had started upward, every old furnace trap in this country, that had been idle for years, was repaired and put to work, and run to its full capacity. All the ore, coal and timber lands were optioned, and every body seemed to be going into the iron business; and, in the spring of 1880, it was plainly to be seen, that there was to be an enormous production of pig-iron.

The fact of the business was, that there were a million of tons more iron made in 1880 than in 1879, and the consequence was, that the up-

ward march in the price had to halt in that year
—and this very over production has ruined the
iron trade, and brought about unprofitable general business to this day.

Take any trade or industry in this country,
where the people are free to engage in it, and
not hampered by any restrictive laws, and the
moment that prices rise in any product or commodity, it seems that every body—like a flock
of sheep—goes in that direction, and we soon
have an over production, and down goes the
price for a number of years. What can be said
of any one production in this respect can be
applied to general business; and no matter if
the country in itself is sound, and the ability of
consumers to absorb and pay for their wants
and luxuries, large emigration and great
growth, the startling fact present itself that
business can and does stagnate and becomes
very much depressed in these repetitions of the
long terms of decline in iron.

Better times can not come for general business, until the price of iron shows that it is in
demand in the industries of this country. And
to answer the above inquiry, the record of the
number of failures is here given, and the ups
and downs in iron in the past and extended into the future, showing how long these numerous
failures must continue.

NO. OF FAILURES.

Year	Failures	
1854		Iron high.
1855		
1856		
1857	4,932	
1858	4,225	
1859	3,913	
1860	8,676	
1861	6,993	Iron low.
1862	1,652	
1863	495	
1864	520	
1865	530	Iron high.
1866	1,505	
1867	2,780	
1868	2,608	
1869	2,799	
1870	8,546	Iron low.
1871	2,915	
1872	4,069	
1873	5,183	Iron high.
1874	5,830	
1875	7,740	
1876	9,092	
1877	8,872	
1878	10,478	Iron low.
1879	6,658	
1880	4,735	Iron high.
1881	5,582	
1882	6,738	
1883	9,184	
1884		
1885		
1886		
1887		
1888		Iron low.

It can be seen, by the foregoing diagram, that whenever iron is high there is a less number of failures, and as iron declines in price, and is low, the failures increase, and reach their greatest number when iron is at its lowest point.

This showing indicates that there will be an increased number of failures, over and above the number for 1883, before we get a turn in business affairs, as we have not reached the lowest limit for iron in this decline.

RAILROAD STOCKS.

The magnitude of the railroad interest of this country, has given it the position of the great leading element for speculation and investment.

This business has grown so extensively in the United States, in the past twenty years, that it excites admiration and wonder.

In 1860 there were only 30,635 miles of finished road, and about 250 members of the New York Stock Exchange. In this year there is over 120,000 miles of road, with over 1,000 members of the New York Exchange.

This great activity in railroad building and stock operations have been the result of the greenback era. With the rapid settlement of the

Western States under land grants, homestead
laws and agricultural machinery began to increase immensely, since the war, the East and
West railroad traffic—there having been built
within the last three years more miles of railroad than was built altogether before the war.
The railroad system being now almost practi-
cally completed east of the Mississippi river,
we can reasonably expect to see the excitement,
pertaining to so many new projected lines pass
away, and the price for railroad stocks to take
their legitmate place in the market, along with
iron, and rise and fall in their value, as iron goes
up and down, in the markets of our country.

The time is past now for any great excitement in the activity and advance in stocks, and,
for a few years following, we may look for continued lower prices, with the exceptions of some
upheavals that may be engineered and produced by combinations and manipulations.

The speculator who may attempt to bull the
stock market, or the investor who may confide
his means in these securities, thinking the turn
has come for another boom in the stock market,
will find, in the long run, that the market will
gradually and surely go away from him—like
the sand from under the feet of the fisherman,
while standing in a stream of running water.

There is a saying in Wall Street that there is one certain way to make money in stocks: "Buy when they are cheap, and sell when they are dear." This is the simplest kind of a rule, and it is a perpetual wonder that so many fail in getting the hang of it.

In Wall Street, it is the operator who forms a correct theory as to the course of prices who makes the most money in the long run—mere traders are sure to get swamped. It is those who see furthest ahead, and have the courage to act upon their convictions, that secure the great prizes in the stock market.

In the year 1860, some of the leading stocks at that time were very low—Erie, 8; New York and Harlem, 8; Michigan Southern, 5; Cleveland and Pittsburgh, 5.

In 1877, some low prices again—Erie, 5; Hannibal & St. Joe, 7; Ohio and Mississippi, $2\frac{1}{2}$; Wabash, $\frac{1}{2}$.

There were two periods, one before the war and the other afterward, when stocks were very low, and those were the times to make investments. The same opportunity for investors to catch stocks so low as in these two years will not, in opinion of the author, come around again until after the next panic, as described in this book; as these two low periods were the effects of the revulsions in business caused by the panics of 1857 and 1873.

In the declines of 1865, 1867, and 1870, we did not have as low prices as after the panic of 1873, when prices for stocks seem to almost vanish out of sight.

In the present decline, from 1881 to 1884, we have something similar to the declines into 1867 and 1870, and some lower points made this year than in 1865, 1867 or 1870, and, reasoning from what we know, stocks have been low enough in this year for this decline so far, and, therefore, we should not have lower points until after next year, the year 1885 being a steady and slightly up year for iron. In the years 1886 and 1887 there will be lower stocks, running into 1888, when the turn comes again for activity in iron stocks and all business.

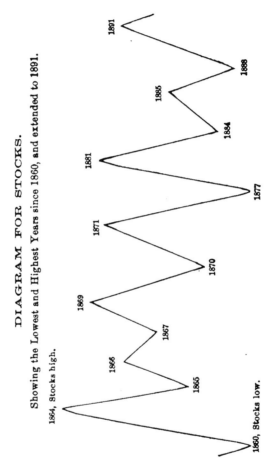

DIAGRAM FOR STOCKS.

Showing the Lowest and Highest Years since 1860, and extended to 1891.

MILES OF RAILROAD IN U. S.

YEAR.	MILES IN OPERATION.	ANNUAL INCREASE.
1820	23	
1831	95	72
1832	229	134
1833	380	151
1834	633	253
1835	1,098	465
1836	1,273	175
1837	1,497	224
1838	1,913	416
1839	2,302	389
1840	2,818	516
1841	3,535	717
1842	4,026	491
1843	4,185	159
1844	4,377	192
1845	4,633	256
1846	4,930	297
1847	5,598	668
1848	5,996	398
1849	7,365	1,369
1850	9,021	1,656
1851	10,982	1,961
1852	12,908	1,926
1853	15,360	2,452
1854	16,720	1,360
1855	18,374	1,654
1856	22,016	3,647
1857	24,503	2,647
1858	26,968	2,465

YEAR.			MILES IN OPERATION.			ANNUAL INCREASE.
1859	.	. .	28,789	.	. .	1,821
1860	.	. .	30,635	.	. .	1,846
1861	.	. .	31,286	.	. .	651
1862	.	. .	32,120	.	. .	834
1863	.	. .	33,170	.	. .	1,050
1864	.	. .	33,908	.	. .	738
1865	.	. .	35,085	.	. .	1,177
1866	.	. .	36,801	.	. .	1,742
1867	.	. .	39,250	.	. .	2,449
1868	.	. .	42,229	.	. .	2,979
1869	.	. .	46,844	.	. .	4,615
1870	.	. .	52,914	.	. .	6,070
1871	.	. ı	60,283	.	. .	7,379
1872	.	. .	66,171	.	. .	5,878
1873	.	. .	70,278	.	. .	4,107
1874	.	. .	72,383	.	. .	2,105
1875	.	. .	74,096	:	. .	1,712
1876	.	. .	76,808	.	. .	2,712
1877	.	. .	79,089	.	. .	2,281
1878	.	. .	81,776	.	. .	2,687
1879	.	. .	86,497	.	. .	4,721
1880	.	. .	91,944	.	. .	7,174
1881	.	. .	101,733	.	. .	9,789
1882	.	. .	113,329	.	. .	11,591

WINTER PACKING OF HOGS—NET AND GROSS COST.

SEASON.	NO. PACKED.	COST. NET.	COST. GROSS.
1842–43	675,000		
1843–44	1,245,000		
1844–45	790,000	$ 3 30	$ 2 65
1845–46	900,000	4 85	3 90
1846–47	800,000	3 55	2 85
1847–48	1,710,000	3 25	2 60
1848–49	1,560,000	4 70	3 75
1849–50	1,652,220	2 66	2 13
1850–51	1,332,867	3 75	3 00
1851–52	1,182,846	4 45	3 56
1852–53	2,201,110	6 01	4 81
1853–54	2,534,770	4 19	3 35
1854–55	2,124,404	4 21	3 37
1855–56	2,489,502	5 75	4 60
1856–57	1,818,468	5 94	4 75
1857–58	2,210,778	4 86	3 89
1858–59	2,465,552	6 28	5 02
1859–60	2,350,822	5 91	4 73
1860–61	2,155,702	5 67	4 57
1861–62	2,893,666	3 03	2 42
1862–63	4,069,520	4 20	3 36
1863–64	3,261,105	6 70	5 36
1864–65	2,442,779	14 32	11 46
1865–66	1,785,955	11 67	9 34
1866–67	2,490,791	7 22	5 78
1867–68	2,781,084	7 95	6 36
1868–69	2,499,873	10 22	8 18
1869–70	2,635,312	11 53	9 22

SEASON.	NO. PACKED.	COST. NET.	COST. GROSS.
1870–71	3,695,251	6 58	5 26
1871–72	4,831,558	5 15	4 12
1872–73	5,410,314	4 66	3 73
1873–74	5,466,200	5 43	4 34
1874–75	5,566,226	8 33	6 60
1875–76	4,880,135	8 82	7 05
1876–77	5,101,308	7 18	5 74
1877–78	6,505,446	4 99	3 99
1878–79	7,480,648	3 56	2 85
1879–80	6,950,451	5 22	4 18
1880–81	6,919,456	5 80	4 64
1881–82	5,747,760	7 58	6 06
1882–83	6,132,212	7 85	6 28

CORN.

YEAR.			PRODUCTION.			AVERAGE VALUE PER BU.
1840	.	.	377,000,000			
1850	.	.	592,000,000			
1860	.	.	838,000,000			
1862	.	.	533,387,230	.	.	34
1863	.	.	397,839,212	.	.	69
1864	.	.	530,451,403	.	.	99
1865	.	.	704,427,853	.	.	46
1866	.	.	867,946,295	.	.	68
1867	.	.	768,420,000	.	.	80
1868	.	.	906,527,000	.	.	62
1869	.	.	874,320,000	.	.	75
1870	.	.	1,094,255,000	.	.	54
1871	.	.	991,898,000	.	.	48
1872	.	.	1,092,719,000	.	.	39
1873	.	.	932,274,000	.	.	48
1874	.	.	850,148,500	.	.	04
1875	.	.	1,321,069,000	.	.	42
1876	.	.	1,283.827,500	.	.	37
1877	.	.	1,342,558,000	.	.	35
1878	.	.	1,388,218,750	.	.	31
1879	.	.	1,547,901,790	.	.	37
1880	.	.	1,717,434,543	.	.	39
1881	.	.	1,194,916,000	.	.	63
1882	.	.	1,617,025,100	.	.	48
1883	.	.	1,500,000,000			

THE WEATHER.

The author does not claim to be a weather prophet, as the weather seems to be one of the most fickle of all things under the sun. However, a chart is here given to show when the scorching heats and droughts, the great floods and prolonged cold winters, have appeared at certain periods in this country, that seem to repeat the order of their return in about every eight years. This order is extended into the future, showing the probabilities of the recurrence of these extremes in the seasons, varying the crops, and affecting the price of corn and hogs.

The extremes of rain-fall and great floods recur at regular periods of about eight years in the Ohio and Mississippi rivers.

The periods of drought and extreme low water occur regularly at almost equal intervals between those of high water.

The repetition of long, cold and stormy winters coincide nearly with those of drought in recurrence and duration.

WEATHER CHART.

	YEARS WET.	YEARS DRY.	
	1850		
Flood.	1851		
	1852		
	1853		
		1854	
		1855	Drought—Low Water.
		1856	Drought—Low Water.
		1857	
	1858		
Flood.	1859		
	1860		
	1861		
		1862	
		1863	Drought—Low Water.
		1864	Drought—Low Water.
		1865	
	1866		
Flood.	1867		
	1868		
	1869		
		1870	
		1871	Drought—Low Water.
		1872	Drought—Low Water.
		1873	
	1874		
Flood.	1875		
	1876		
	1877		
		1878	
		1879	Drought—Low Water.
		1880	
		1881	Drought--Low Water.

	1882	
Flood.	1883	
	1884	
	1885	
	1886	
	1887	Drought—Low Water.
	1888	Drought—Low Water.
	1889	
	1890	
Flood.	1891	
	1892	
	1893	

The weather chart is designed to show, first, on the right, the group of four years of extreme heat and extreme cold; and second, on the left, four years of heavy rain-falls and great floods.

The author does not claim that all the years in the groups on the right of the chart will be years of drought and heat and cold winters; neither will all those years on the left be years of excessive rain-fall.

It is only asserted that there will be two of these years on the right of extreme heat and cold winters, and on the left at least one regularly returning year, in which there will be a great flood, as pointed out on the chart.

On the right, in the first group of four years, there were extensive droughts in 1855 and 1856; and the winters of 1855–56 and 1856–57 were extremely cold.

In the second group, there were extensive

droughts in 1863 and 1864, and the winters of 1863–64 and 1864–65 were extremely cold.

In the third group there were extensive droughts in 1871 and 1872; and the winters of 1871–72 and 1872–73 were extremely cold.

In the fourth group there wore extensive droughts in 1879 and 1881, and the winters of 1878–9 and 1880–81 were extremely cold.

On the left, in the first group of four years, there was a great flood in 1851.

In the second group there was a great flood in 1859. In the third group there was a great flood in 1867.

In the fourth group there was a great flood in 1875. In the fifth group there was a great flood in 1883.

From these records of the past thirty years, without going back to hunt down far-fetched data, the conclusions and probabilities are, that there will not be any very great floods in our rivers from this time till after 1889, with the exception of the year 1886 (when heretofore there has been high waters the first year of these groups of dry years), and, after passing the Spring of 1886, the river population can be assured of no extraordinary floods of high water till 1890 and 1891.

Also, that there will not be any general

droughts extending all over this country, with extreme heat, till after 1886; and that there will not be any excessive, prolonged cold winters until 1887.

For the next two years, average seasons of rain-fall, gradually decreasing till 1887 and 1888, when in these years there will be general droughts and low water in the rivers.

The winters of 1837–88 and 1888–89, will be extreme prolonged cold winters, with storms of snow.

After 1888, the rain-fall will gradually increase till 1891, when there will be a great flood in the Ohio and Mississippi rivers.

The year 1889 will be grasshopper year for the States and Territories West of the Mississippi river.

STAGES OF THE OHIO RIVER AT CINCINNATI, OHIO.

[*From the Report of the Chamber of Commerce.*]

YEAR.	HIGHEST. Ft. In.	LOWEST. Ft. In.	AVERAGE. Ft. In.
1832	64. 3		
1847	63. 7		
1858	43.10	2. 5	12.10
1859	55. 5	3. 3	17. 7
1860	49. 2	5. 4	16.
1861	49. 5	5. 1	19. 1
1862	57. 4	2. 4	17. 5
1863	42. 9	2. 6	15.
1864	45. 1	3. 1	16. 8

1865	56. 3	5. 8	21.10
1866	42. 6	4. 9	19. 2
1867	55. 8	3.	17.
1868	48. 3	5. 1	18. 8
1869	48. 9	5. 4	19. 8
1870	55. 3	3.10	17.10
1871	40. 6	2. 8	11.10
1872	41. 9	3.	11. 8
1873	44. 5	3. 8	18. 5
1874	47.11	2. 4	15. 8
1875	55. 4	4. 3	18. 9
1876	51. 9	6. 2	18. 2
1877	53. 9	3. 3	15.
1878	41. 4	4. 4	16. 9
1879	42. 9	2. 6	14. 6
1880	53. 2	3. 9	17.
1881	50. 7	1.11	16.11
1882	58. 7	6. 1	22. 1½
1883	66. 4	3. 7	19. 5¼
1884	71. 0¾		

CORN AND HOGS.

The price of corn and hogs is moved up and down more quickly in their repetitions, by the changes in the weather and seasons, than the price of some manufactured commodities; for instance iron, which takes a longer term of years to bring about a large or small supply, as the cycle in hogs is only from five to six years, while iron a much longer term of years.

In the repetitions of the ups and downs as given in this book, the low price for 1877 was continued into 1878, by the dread of resumption of specie payments, which resulted in keeping prices down into 1878 for hogs, iron, and other commodities.

The last high year for hogs was fixed for 1880. Now to assign a reason why the price continued to advance, after that year to 1882, for corn and hogs.

It can only be charged to the great drought of 1881 not coming in the year 1880, its proper place.

The former regularly returning droughts, as shown in the weather chart (which is introduced here for this purpose), were in the years 1855–56, 1863–64, 1871–72, 1879, skipping 1880, the high priced year in the cycle, and giving us the drought in 1881, which was an excessive dry summer, partially destroying the corn crop.

This delayed disastrous drought being preceded by the extraordinary long continued cold of the winter of 1880–81, which had already thinned out a great number of hogs, was the direct cause of the high prices being continued longer than the cycle denoted.

The low point for corn and hogs is for this winter; that is, for the packing season of 1883–84, which no doubt will show a lower average price than for the packing season of 1882–'83.

The further prophecies are for a higher

average after this winter, till the packing season of 1886-87.

Now, to maintain prices about the present
level, or to have a higher average for the next
three years, there must be some failures in the
corn or hog crops; and reasoning from what
we know, that during the cold January of this
winter the young hogs have died in considerable
numbers. And in accordance with that which
our weather chart indicates, the summer seasons
for a couple of years, will be wet, with low tem-
perature, and not favorable for large yields of
merchantable sound corn. And the further indications are, that we will not have good corn
crops until the dry weather of 1887 and 1888,
when the price of corn and hogs will decline to
a lower average, as they did during the dry
weather of 1871 and 1872.

HIGHEST AND LOWEST PRICES IN NEW YORK FOR
MIDDLING UPLAND COTTON AND THE CROPS:

YEAR.	HIGHEST.	LOWEST.	BALES.
1826	14	9	—— ——
1827	12	8	—— ——
1828	13	9	—— ——
1829	11	8	—— ——
1830	13	8	—— ——
1831	11	7	987,477
1832	12	7	1,070,438
1833	17	9	1,205,394
1834	16	10	1,254,328
1835	20	15	1,360,725
1836	20	12	1,425,575
1837	17	7	1,804,797
1838	12	9	1,363,403
1839	16	11	2,181,749
1840	10	8	1,639,353
1841	11	9	1,688,675
1842	9	7	2,394,203
1843	8	5	2,108,579
1844	9	5	2,484,662
1845	9	. 4	2,170,537
1846	9	6	1,860,479
1847	12	7	2,424,113
1848	8	5	2,808,596
1849	11	6	2,171,706

1850	14	11	2,415,257
1851	14	8	3,090,029
1852	10	8	3,352,882
1853	11	10	3,035,027
1854	10	8	2,932,339
1855	11	7	3,645,345
1856	12	9	3,056,519
1857	15	13	3,238,902
1858	13	9	3,994,481
1859	12	11	4,823,770
1860 ·	11	10	3,826,086
1861	28	11	———
1862	68	20	———
1863	88	54	———
1864	1.90	72	———
1865	1.22	33	2,228,987
1866	52	32	2,059,271
1867	36	$15\frac{1}{2}$	2,498,895
1868	33	16	2,439,039
1869	35	25	3,154,946
1870	$25\frac{3}{4}$	15	4,352,317
1871	$21\frac{1}{4}$	$14\frac{3}{4}$	2,974,351
1872	$27\frac{3}{8}$	$18\frac{5}{8}$	3,930,508
1872	$21\frac{3}{8}$	$1?\frac{5}{8}$	4,170,388
1874	$18\frac{7}{8}$	$14\frac{3}{4}$	3,832,991
1875	$17\frac{1}{8}$	$13\frac{1}{16}$	4,669,288
1876	$13\frac{3}{8}$	$10\frac{5}{8}$	4,485,423
1877	$13\frac{5}{16}$	$10\frac{3}{16}$	4,773,865
1878	$12\frac{3}{16}$	$8\frac{13}{16}$	5,074,155
1879	$13\frac{1}{4}$	$9\frac{1}{4}$	5,761,252
1880	$13\frac{1}{4}$	$10\frac{5}{16}$	6,605,750
1881	13	$10\frac{7}{16}$	5,456,048
1882	$13\frac{1}{16}$	$10\frac{1}{4}$	———

WHEAT.

YEAR.			PRODUCTION.			AVERAGE VALUE PER BU.	
1862	.	.	177.957,172	.	.	$	93
1863	.	.	173,677.928	.	.	1	14
1864	.	.	160,695,823	.	.	1	83
1865	.	.	148,522.827	.	.	1	46
1866	.	.	151.999 906	.	.	2	19
1867	.	.	212,441,400	.	.	1	98
1868	.	.	224,036,600	.	.	1·	42
1869	.	.	260,146,900	.	.		91
1870	.	.	235,884,700	.	.	1	04
1871	.	.	230,722,400	.	.	1	25
1872	.	.	249,997,100	.	.	1	24
1873	.	.	281,254,700	.	.	1	15
1874	.	.	309.102,700	.	.		94
1875	.	.	292,126,000	.	.	1	00
1876	.	.	289,356,500	.	.	1	03
1877	.	.	364,194.146	.	.	1	08
1878	.	.	420,122.400	.	.		77
1879	.	.	448,756,630	.	.	1	10
1880	.	.	498,549,868	.	.		95
1881	.	.	380,280,090	.	.	1	19
1882	.	.	504,185,470	.	.		88
1883	.	.	420,000,000				

The total production and average value per bushel of the wheat crops since 1862, are here given as compiled by the Department of Agriculture.

The author has never been enabled to form any cycles in the price of this cereal that would show any repetition of high or low prices that could be extended into the future.

To judge of the surrounding conditions and circumstances, such as large visible supplies in this country and Europe, and the known large quantities in farmers' granaries, and good prospects for a large yield of the growing winter wheat—with a greatly lessened demand from foreign countries compared with the past few years—and the existing depression in general business in this country. These prospective supplies and probable demand indicate, that this country will have *cheap bread* for this year, 1884.

February 25th, 1884.

Printed in the United States
122892LV00004B/91/A